Cancer

A Journey's End

Prashant Naik

Matador
9 Priory Business Park,
Wistow Road, Kibworth Beauchamp,
Leicestershire. LE8 0RX
Tel: (+44) 116 279 2299
Fax: (+44) 116 279 2277
Email: books@troubador.co.uk
Web: www.troubador.co.uk/matador

ISBN 978 1785899 669

British Library Cataloguing in Publication Data.
A catalogue record for this book is available from the British Library.

Printed by TJ International, Padstow, Cornwall, UK
Typeset in 11pt Adobe Garamond Pro by Troubador Publishing Ltd, Leicester, UK

Matador is an imprint of Troubador Publishing Ltd

I dedicate this book
to my two beautiful girls,
Kira and Anjali, whose strength and courage
have been an inspiration.

And to my beautiful wife, Tanvi,
who fought the good fight of faith
and will always remain in my heart
for the rest of my days
and beyond.

INTRODUCTION

Tanvi and I were brought up in two very different environments. I was born and raised in the UK, and Tanvi in India. We both hail from Hindu families and our mother tongue is Gujarati. Our coming together was through an arranged marriage. The term 'arranged' is a bit misleading; it is more of an introduction to be honest. If a potential bride is not interested in a groom then that is the end of that, and vice versa. We were married in 1998 on the 20th April in India and Indian weddings are never small; around 1500 people attended, which included the majority of my family from the UK. For Tanvi, arriving in the UK wasn't easy: she found it very difficult at the beginning to settle, due to our lifestyle, which is rather different in comparison to living in India. However, slowly but steadily she adjusted and we moved on. Tanvi was a no-nonsense type of person; if she had a goal in mind she was going to achieve it and nothing was going to get in the way. I can only describe Tanvi as feisty, but underneath she had a soft, tender core that only I witnessed. Regarding her career, Tanvi had a choice: she already had a BSc in Chemistry, so all she had to do was one year's extra study to meet the standards and she could start working. However, Tanvi had other ideas: she also had a Masters in Law & Labour Welfare and she was keen to study law; to do this meant five years of part-time study. We thought long and hard about this and I said if she really wanted to do this, I would support her. It did mean that it would be a while before we could afford a house – due to the cost of living and house prices, two incomes were necessary – but we looked at the bigger picture. Long term it would be better for both of us, and future kids. Therefore, as we agreed, within a year, Tanvi worked on her English and went to university to study law.

In 2003, my life took a dramatic change: that year, I gave my life to Christ. I was always interested in the idea of a God but never really believed in anything. Hinduism to me was too complicated, but Christianity seemed simple: you had God and then there was this person named Jesus, that was it. It was only later on that I learned about the aspects of the Holy Spirit. Therefore, why change? What propelled me to take a leap of faith? It was the pressures of life; I felt burdened and stressed, money was tight – that didn't help – and we were living with my parents so we had to get on to the property ladder. At the time I was the only one earning, so that wasn't going to happen any time soon. Therefore, there I was one night watching TV on my own, flicking from channel to channel. I came across the God Channel and was watching a man called Steve Hill preaching the Gospel. I sat there thinking *I quite like this* so I devised a plan as to at what point I would become a Christian. I figured it would be boring, so I planned to enjoy the rest of my life and then, when I was old and about to kick the bucket, I would give my life to Christ; that to me seemed like a plan.

I thought nothing of it and the next day I continued my TV-watching ritual and the same person was on again. However, this time I was in for a surprise. I sat there feeling quite clever about myself and the great plan I had devised, when suddenly, Steve Hill, the preacher, turned to the camera and said, "If you think you can spend the rest of your life enjoying yourself and then come to God, you'd better think twice; what's to say you won't live to see another day?" Those words shook me to the core. He was speaking to me; how did he know? I stood up and turned the telly off. I went upstairs, walked into the bathroom, locked the door, got on my knees, and gave my life to Christ.

Unlike me, Tanvi was a devout Hindu. She understood a lot more than me, in fact growing up we just did what our parents told us; ignorance was bliss as far as we were concerned. Tanvi gave her life to Christ nearly four years later, in spite of my wayward preaching: when you're new to Christianity sometimes you think you know it all; my preaching was just that – long and preachy. I am amazed I didn't put her off completely; I wasn't a complete disaster; I just didn't know when to shut up. Four years later, one evening, I decided to do something that I should have done years ago, I just asked the Lord what I was doing wrong. He said "Walk in love." I thought about this and dwelled on this for a while. I also got a sense that the Holy Spirit was telling me to just tell Tanvi how much God loved her and nothing else. So for the next two weeks that's all I did; if she was frustrated I would just tell her that God loved her and that was it. I felt inside that it wasn't going to cut it; where was the long sermon on the consequences of not being with Christ, the brimstone and fire? However, I also sensed the Holy Spirit saying, "Now shut up". Two weeks later, she gave her life to Christ; I wasn't even at home, I was at work. Now we were literally singing from the same hymn book; now we could move forward and everything would be fine.

LIFE'S ABOUT TO TAKE A NASTY TURN

It was around 23rd June 2012; we had just planned Mom's birthday party, and we had never had a birthday party for Mom so Tanvi and I decided to throw her a surprise party. We had just moved into our own house so we were looking forward to throwing this party. It was a great day, Mom was totally surprised and shocked to see all our family members crammed into our house; everyone had a great day.

Little did we know what was around the corner and the impact it would have on our lives and everyone else around us; we had everything, two great kids and a lovely house. We had only moved into the area in October 2010, things were looking up for the both of us.

As Christians, we were always thankful to the Lord for all that we had. All our achievements we had gained, we always thanked the Lord for, we could never lay claim that it was down to our ability, because we knew he gives us the ability to succeed in life as long as we are willing to put in the effort.

It was roughly a week later; Tanvi had just entered her period cycle, nothing new there, she would be snappy as usual; you tend to get used to these mood swings, you just stay out of the way. However, she called me up as she had noticed a hardening of the left breast, it was as if a solid ball was inside her left breast. This had happened last time as well so we decided to wait until she had finished her cycle; if there was no change then we would go and get it checked out. We prayed that night however, the tension and worry was always there in the back of our minds.

We both mentally counted down the days to see if there was any change, however this time, the hardness remained. As I gazed at Tanvi I could see the tension in her face; Tanvi was never one for hiding her emotions. I suppose we were both the same in that respect. I comforted her and told her not to worry, trust the Lord and we would be ok, we would get it checked out and I was sure everything would be fine. That didn't help much; I could see the worry on her face, and a few words of comfort were never going to wash it all away.

First thing Monday morning, we went to the GP's. After being checked by the local nurse, she recommended that Tanvi see a specialist at the hospital, so she booked us in for a visit in two weeks. Frankly, two weeks was not quick enough; we needed to know fast, so I informed the nurse that I had private health cover. One of the best things I ever did was getting private cover through my work; this covered not only Tanvi but the girls and me as well, and so a letter was drafted, which I picked up the next day. I immediately opened a case through the private health company and set about finding the best private hospital I could find that was near us. Time was of the utmost importance; if we had to travel a bit then so be it. I managed to get an appointment through Spire Healthcare in Solihull within two days. This seemed to lessen the tension that was building up by now as Tanvi was already fearing the worst. I was concerned as well but you always try to reason things out and, of course, it doesn't happen to you, it's always someone else, so we had nothing to worry about, we would be okay, everything would be fine – so I kept telling myself.

It was Thursday and off we went to the hospital, still hoping that all would be well, that it was probably just hormonal or menopause, anything but what we feared. After a brief consultation the surgeon sent Tanvi up for a biopsy; he suggested that this was the best thing to do and he was slightly concerned about the situation. After the biopsy was done we waited, then we were called in; you only had to see the doctor's face to realise that this was serious. We sat down and braced ourselves. After giving us all the medical jargon, our worst fears were confirmed: it was cancer. Tanvi immediately broke down, I did my best to comfort her and said that we had fought battles before. In 2010, I suffered from pneumonia, which developed in to bronchiectasis, which meant my lungs were carrying water thus reducing my capacity to breathe. I lost two stone in a month during that period, which really tested us both, and in 2012, I spent eight weeks off work after hip surgery; so you see it's not as if we were unaccustomed to trouble, and I hoped that we would get through this one as well. However, you can only stay strong for so long before the situation overtakes you. I cracked for a brief moment, but I was determined to stand by her side and be as strong as possible. This would be a recurring pattern that would follow me throughout this journey; you can only stay strong for so long then you fall, and at times when you fall under the weight of it, all the people around you suffer as well.

The surgeon needed to know the full extent of the problem, as he wanted to know how far this had gone, so Tanvi went for a full CT scan, an MRI scan and a bone scan. I was about to learn quite a lot about this illness and how it can affect the body. The doctor explained that a specialist would be assigned for her chemotherapy treatment. The treatment would be determined via a committee of three to four consultants; this was common practice to cover all possibilities that could arise.

Therefore, we left the hospital stunned, naturally reeling from the news. Now it was a case of telling the rest of the family; telling the girls their mom had cancer. I started by ringing my brother; if there's one person I know who won't fall apart on me, it's him. We had already told family members that we were going for tests, and why; that was only immediate family members as there was no point getting everybody else involved as we wanted to keep things as normal as possible. One by one, we told those who needed to know, and I left it to my brother to get to my place and tell Mom and Dad, because I didn't have the heart and I needed to compose myself. I think we both cried all the way home that morning, finally establishing some kind of composure by the time we got home. Of course, our respective employers needed to know. Tanvi worked for

HSBC and I worked for Fujitsu Services; both employees proved to be supportive throughout, removing any form of pressure from Tanvi and me. We got home and Mom was already in tears; we all broke down and comforted each other. The girls came home that day from school and I sat down with them and explained the situation. Kira started to cry immediately; Anjali, being the youngest, didn't fully understand – not surprising as she was only eight years old at the time. We decided we would involve the girls throughout, as much as possible, without telling them information that would upset them too much. It's a fine line with kids, how much you tell them, what they need to know etc.

It took a while but Tanvi and I started to pick ourselves up, talking positively about the treatment, and how so many people get through this and how we would as well. I'd never met such a strong-willed woman as Tanvi; she was determined that we were going to beat this, so much so that she went to work on the Monday leaving her work colleagues totally shocked. Tanvi was determined to work for as long as she could and no one was going to stop her. Frankly, they were wise to just listen to her, but there were times where she needed to be reminded to slow down, so naturally I would curtail her enthusiasm to work and speak directly with her managers to determine her working hours, as they had to be reduced. Tanvi was informed what hours she was going to work and that was it. I exchanged numbers with her managerial line so they knew her condition at home, just in case she got too over-keen regarding work. They were brilliant with me; if I told them that she hadn't slept well on any particular night I would let them know, without Tanvi knowing. That way we could keep her in check, stopping her from getting carried away. Sometimes I would let them know it might be a good idea to let her go home early due to the previous day's exertions.

My life was about to change drastically, it was about to get consumed with one thing only: her treatment and cancer; everything else was a sideshow. Nothing could ever prepare me for what I was about to go through mentally, physically and spiritually; my faith was about to be tested on a level that I would only fully understand a few years later.

I had worked for Fujitsu Services for thirteen years, carrying out several jobs within the company. However, my own career was about to change: before all this treatment, I had been looking to move into another department, with higher pay and better prospects hopefully. I didn't have the best of times in the job I was currently doing; for several years I had managed, and that was my strong point; doing a technical role did not best suit me. When you have managed for so long, taking orders was something I needed to get used to and frankly, I wasn't the best at this all the time. I really knew how to test my own faith when it came to obedience in the workplace and what the Bible said on this area, and test my Team Leader's resolve. However, this was not the time for moving; I needed stability, and staying in my current role was the best thing to do. On top of that, I worked with a great bunch of people, who were supportive and helped me through some difficult times.

That weekend was a long weekend for us, I had to

tell my father-in-law that their daughter had cancer, but I bottled it as I didn't have the courage to tell him myself. I felt as if I had failed in some way and this thought process would continue to build throughout the next two years. I spoke to Tanvi's aunt, whom I was a lot closer to, who, in turn, spoke to Tanvi's parents.

We prayed about our situation and both of us got our lives right with God; we trusted the Lord and as we built ourselves up in the Word we started to focus on what needed to be done. We hadn't been going to a church for a while since we moved, and I didn't feel led in any way to run to church now. However, in hindsight, you need a strong base of friends and family around you; don't try to deal with it all yourselves, it's an impossible task and you will only load more pressure on yourselves.

GOING BACK TO
WORK ON MONDAY

I needed to go to work; they already knew the situation as we had spoken on the phone and I had briefed them on the Friday after we got back home. As I walked into the office, people's heads dropped; it's difficult when you are placed in a situation when someone who you work with is going through this type of illness: you don't know what to say. Those who had experienced this type of illness in their families and friends were the first to come and see me. A friend of mine who sat right opposite me, who had lost his father to cancer so this resonated with him, struggled to even look at me. As I'm sure a lot was going through his mind regarding his dad, I felt for him so I made an effort to just go and lighten the situation as much as possible. Carl did his best to act normal and I appreciated that. It would take Carl at least a week before things were okay between the two of us; I gave him all the space he needed and did my best to show that I was strong and all was well. I tried my best to make the atmosphere in the office as normal as possible, putting people at ease, because it can get a bit awkward at times. Humour has always been a way for me to get through difficult times, however it didn't always work out well; let's just say my sense of humour is an acquired taste. I got a laugh out of it so that was good enough for me.

After a meeting with my bosses, they decided to take away a lot of my project work and lighten my load. I was happy with that; I had managed staff before myself and I realised that sometimes, when you have people going through stuff at home, their work life can be affected. We sat down and discussed what the doctors had said. Mike Swales, who was and currently is my Ops Manager, was fantastic; he gave me his full support, along with my two Team Leaders, Kiran Katakia and Mali Khangura. Their support was second to none all the way through and I will always be grateful for that.

Our next step was our first appointment with the chemo consultant; we discussed all the types of treatment that Tanvi was going to have to go through: eight rounds of chemo, a mastectomy and fourteen days of radiotherapy. This was quite intense and it covered a period from August 2012 to January 2013. It was important that she had the chemotherapy first, as there was no way they could have performed the surgery first, due to the breast being so hard and having no flexibility at all. This was quite a heavy load and a lot to take in especially for Tanvi, who didn't like needles. I remember a time after she first came to the UK when she had to give blood for a test, routine stuff, and she started crying, and frankly I couldn't stop laughing; it was quite ridiculous and embarrassing.

The nurse then briefed Tanvi about what she was going to have to go through; first she discussed all the different possible side effects that she may face, as each patient will react differently to the treatment. I continued to listen, and then it was my turn. The nurse took one look at me and said, "And you're the one who's going to get it in the neck." I raised my eyebrows and thought to myself, *What have I done?* What she meant was, this was going to be challenging for Tanvi. When she was angry, frustrated and moody, I would be the one she would take it out on. And boy, did I get it in the neck.

It didn't take long for the pressure to start building. I didn't realise it at the time, but it was there, like a snowball down a hill, slowly building up, frustration, anger, confusion, the constant reminders of what meds to take at what time, all this building up in me. Tanvi's medicine sheet looked like a school timetable, Monday to Friday, morning session to afternoon session and night session. This was a lot to take in and what didn't help was that my memory was not the best, to Tanvi's frustration.

I have always been the type of person who needed to know in advance what I was going to do and how I would deal with a problem. A plan for everything, that's me. Once Tanvi was diagnosed, I entered a realm which I had no control over, I couldn't plan this one out, just a load of probabilities of what lay ahead, and trying to figure them out was tiring. Now the pressure was building; I was waiting for someone to hand me a guide book on how to deal with the situation, a plan of action. The girls had a booklet on cancer called *Mommy's Little Lump*. It told them how Mom and Dad would deal with this lump, what would happen to Mommy's hair, how Mommy would get angry at times, and sad, how Dad would also do the same. For a child it was a story to read. I read it first and I got a glimpse of what was to come. *So the kids have this guide*, I thought to myself, *where's mine? Who is going to show me how to get through this?* As it turned out, no one; this was one journey I going to have to make up as I went along.

KEY PEOPLE IN
OUR LIVES – OUR HEROES

In situations like this, you need some kind of support structure; someone, or a group of people, who were going to support you and understand your situation as well as possible. Tony and Janine Pearson were two people who we got to know when our eldest, Kira, started at Blackwood Primary School. Both Kira and Maddi were in the same class and have been great friends ever since, and still are, well into their secondary school years. We built up a great friendship with the Pearsons, enjoying a few evenings together as they were a great couple. Once Tony and Janine found out about Tanvi's condition they immediately went about ensuring that all we had to worry about was Tanvi's treatment. If the girls ever needed a break or Tanvi and I wanted to spend some time together, they would take both my girls around to their house so they could spend some time with their friends. The Pearsons have in total three children, Maddi, being the eldest, Libby, and Phe, the youngest. Their support throughout Tanvi's treatment was the best, they stood by our side when we needed it the most and I will always be eternally grateful. Even to this day, a few years later, they continue to support me and the girls. Janine will do the school run in the morning and every now and then will take Kira shopping when needed, to help me out. You don't find quality people like this every day. There are some debts that can't be repaid, and the debt I owe these beloved friends of mine cannot be paid back in my lifetime. All I can say is 'thank you' from the bottom of my heart.

At this time, Kira had started secondary school and Anjali was still at primary; both Blackwood Primary School and The Streetly Academy were outstanding when it came to supporting my girls. Our biggest fear was that, in all that we were about to go through, the girls would be neglected and their education would suffer. However, both schools had experience in dealing with this situation and knew how to deal with any issues that would arise. I was highly blessed by Blackwood Primary School who had access to counsellors ready to step in and deal with any issues that needed to be dealt with. The staff within the schools were amazing and throughout, both schools made sure that the girls were taken care of. I only had to deal with one school, as the primary school head decided that, to save me having to speak to both schools, they would inform the secondary school of any new changes in our situation if required. Even small things like reminder letters for events or key dates the girls had to remember, they said I didn't have to worry about; if they needed anything from me they would call instead. This again was a blessing, it was great to know the girls were looked after and a great weight was lifted off our shoulders. Once again, we thank both schools for their unequivocal support during this time and are grateful for everything they have done for us.

My family members were there for me as well so we weren't alone through this. However, there are always moments when you feel as if it's a battle that only you and your partner fully understand, because let's face it, it's you who is going through it, not them. No one can grasp the enormity of a situation until you walk it yourself.

THE WORKPLACE

At work, it was important that I had the right people around me; while I was grateful for the support from all, I needed people around me who I could talk with. When you go through an experience like this, you need people with experience to talk with. During this time my approach to all situations was, I would say, very abrupt: if you have no life experience in this area, don't bother speaking to me because, with all due respect, you don't know what you are talking about. I didn't need sympathy, I needed someone who had walked this journey or at least had some form of experience in one form or another, someone who had tasted what the pressure was like. Sandra King is a work friend and colleague of mine; her contribution over the first six months was invaluable. Sandra had lost her sister to cancer, roughly six years ago from the writing of this book, so she knew what it was like, and she understood the pain and mental anguish that you go through, that feeling of helplessness and being out of control at times. I immediately connected with Sandra and recognised her grief, building a strong relationship with her; at lunch we would go for walks and talk about all things, she would also ask about how Tanvi was doing and would explain things to me about how I would feel and what she might be going through. Sandra was brilliant; everything she said resonated with me, she seemed to know exactly how I felt and was able to anticipate and draw on her past experience, thus understanding what I might be feeling. Sandra was my outlet, someone to share with, and someone who understood to some degree my situation; she was there for me to release whatever tension and stress that was building up in me.

SEPTEMBER

It was around September 2012 and Tanvi's treatment was well under way – four different types of chemo – the first type, she handled well, there seemed to be no major side effects, all was looking good. What was pleasing throughout her treatment was how she would spend the time in her Bible. Treatment, if I recall, would take about two hours, sometimes slightly longer, but each treatment she spent with her head in her Bible, reading and learning the word of God. It was great to see; she was growing spiritually and understanding more about God's love for her. During this time, I started to see her change from a strong independent woman to a God-dependant woman, getting to know her creator and loving him more and more. Sometimes she would stop and ponder; you could see her meditating on a scripture she had come across or she would stop and ask me a question on what a certain scripture meant. It was what I had always wanted Tanvi to do, to grow in the Lord's word, trust in him and to learn to lean on him. I gave my life to Christ back in 2003 and Tanvi came to know the Lord in 2007, so I had a bit of a head start on her. At my previous church, I spent a lot of time in service doing whatever I could to help where possible; I eventually reached the position of being on the Board of Directors for a period of three years. I didn't think I was qualified to be in that position, but there I was. Maybe the Lord placed me there to learn and grow, but placed in a position like that you soon realise how tough a Senior Pastor's job is, constantly under demand from all quarters. When you start out as a Christian you tend to look at the Senior Pastor's position and think, *That would be good, you get to preach the Word of God*. Then once on the Board and having the ear of the Senior Pastor, you soon realise the Senior Pastor's job is not one you really want to do. As far as I was concerned, it's double the trouble: people expect you to be perfect, whiter than white, but it's impossible, these people are still human, they make mistakes, they are not perfect, only Jesus is perfect, his is the only cup that is full, and yet with Pastors the constant demand on their lives is for all to see.

Going back to the treatment, we knew that, after twenty days, Tanvi's hair would start to fall out. Tanvi had beautiful long black hair; to her it was important that her hair was right, and now she was going to have to go through the trauma of watching her hair fall out as the days went on. Sure enough, as we got to around eighteen days we could gradually see this difficult period take shape. It didn't come out in lumps, thankfully, but as she combed it or if she ran her hands through her hair, a decent amount would fall out. Sometimes she would wake up in the morning and her hair would be all over her pillow. She must have been combing her hair in her car as it was all over the place. The distress on her face said it all; she would look at me with a worried look with hair in her hands. I did my best to help her and console her; in fact, all I would end up doing was make the situation worse. I would tell her not to worry, it would grow back; my tone was supportive, trying not to cause distress. She would just flip! She ripped into me one day, telling me, what did I know? And did I know how long her hair was? And that it would take years to grow back? I should have just taken a grenade and swallowed it, that would have been less damaging; she was just hurting and I knew that. There is not much you can say when you have just been fed to the lions, you just take it, and you become the punchbag.

It was days like this I would go into work and speak to Sandra and she would console me, yet explain that Tanvi was just hurting. I said to her that I could not understand the issue of losing her hair, let's face it, it would grow back and I was right. Sandra would agree that, yes, it would grow back, however I was also wrong. A woman's hair is her crowning glory; for Tanvi, I knew that was true. I was more concerned about the mastectomy; that was my major stress as it was due in November. I was really struggling with that, but Tanvi was not bothered; as far as she was concerned, she could have cosmetic surgery; she even contemplated going a cup bigger.

VISIT TO PINK

The time had come to remove her hair; part of Tanvi's treatment involved information about who were best suited to dealing with cancer patients and we were recommended a company called Pink, who were specialists in hair replacement. We informed the girls that Mom was going to have her hair shaved off to prepare them for what was to come. I took it upon myself to notify the girls, as Tanvi was just not up to it. Kira started to cry about how beautiful Mom's hair was and that she was not happy about it at all. I spent plenty of time with her, letting her know that Mom's hair would grow back and that Mom would be wearing a wig. Tanvi and I had already been to see Pink previously to sort out a wig; I left the choice to her whether she wore the wig or not. The next choice was synthetic or real hair; as far as Tanvi was concerned it was going to be real hair; that was not cheap but I wasn't about to go cheap on her: anything to ensure she was happy. Tanvi decided that she wanted a long hair wig; this was because she had only told her immediate team members about her condition so she had to have long hair to keep up the appearance that nothing was wrong. I, on the other hand, had decided that it was best that all who worked with me in my area knew what was going on. My reason for this was simple: it was purely for protection, not for me, but for them.

In any office environment, you always have some form of banter; that's expected, and sometimes boundaries are crossed, which is normal. On any given day without any issues or stresses, if someone wound me up the wrong way, if I was having a bad day, I would let them know; so imagine the situation where, in the current climate and with the high levels of stress I was feeling, someone pressed all my wrong buttons. I tell you now I would not have liked to be in their shoes. Therefore, it was best that everyone knew what was going on, not in detail but just knew; that way people would think twice about winding me up. I realised it would have been unfair if someone had aggravated me and I had flipped with them not knowing my situation, so I played it safe. Everyone was great with me and gave me my space when I needed it.

Therefore, we arrived at Pink, and a team of women greeted her and we went into the room; once in the room they started to prepare Tanvi and told her that they would only start when she was ready. This was not about going in and having your hair cut, but ensuring that she was comfortable and ready; they would explain to her exactly how they would proceed. Tanvi looked apprehensive. I told her not to worry, she quipped back, "That was easy for you to say," in a firm but strong voice. I said, "Ok, I'll just go sit in the waiting room if you want." She quickly turned and said, "You are staying in this room with me," with a loving look in her eyes. She needed me by her side and I knew that, while she acted strong on the outside, inside she needed the support, so I sat down in the corner and watched as they started to remove her hair. Tanvi was not allowed to sit in front of the mirror, as it can distress the patient during the process. Each time they removed a section they checked her to ensure she was okay; she would ask me how it looked every now and then, I would reassure her that it was looking good. Finally they finished; I could not believe how good she actually looked. I'm not just saying that, her crown was so well proportioned. I smiled at her; she looked just as beautiful with or without hair. "You look great," I said. She wanted to look in the mirror and as she looked I could see her eyes started to fill up, a tear ran down her face, she asked me if I really liked it. At this point the staff left us to give her time to adjust. I held her in my arms and said it was great while wiping a tear from her face. I told her she looked like Persis Khambatta. Persis Khambatta was an Indian model, actress and author. She was best known for her role as Lieutenant Ilia in the 1979 feature film, *Star Trek: The Motion Picture*. She had a perfectly shaped head and was a highly attractive woman with no hair.

I told Tanvi it was quite a sexy look for her; she replied with, "Calm down". I admired Tanvi's courage and took every opportunity to build her up spiritually, and her self-esteem. While this was going on, in the other room they had prepared her wig. I was amazed at how good the wig was, she was not allowed to put any highlights in her wig but you could hardly tell if it was hers or not. Everywhere we went no one could tell, it was that good, so she was pleased. Well, it seemed so at first.

On the surface, Tanvi looked fine, she seemed to be handling the hair loss well, but something was not right as she kept tinkering with it. "It's not right, it's not exactly how I want it," she would say, so I said "Okay, if you want to go back you can, but do it on Saturday." I wanted her to think about it; it looked fine to me, I was very pleased but, hey, she was not happy, so let us go back. I was pleased with the wig, I took a photo and showed it to a few people at work, Sandra, Pinar and Mali, and they said it looked great. Therefore, Saturday came along and I dropped her off asking her how long it would take. "About thirty minutes at most, but I will call you." "Okay," I said. So I went home and went about doing whatever. Three hours later, still no call; something was up, so I called her. She complained it was not right; they just can't get it right. Then the penny dropped: this had nothing to do with the wig but it had everything to do with the ordeal of losing her own hair; the trauma of that experience was festering inside her. I told her I was coming to get her. What I walked into was a room full of staff that looked scared out of their wits. These people are trained to deal with cancer patients and the sensitivity of it all, but it seemed Tanvi had pushed their limits to the full. I was embarrassed; I took one look at them and asked, "Where is she?" They said, "In there." One of the hairdressers tried to explain to me that they had tried everything; her face cried for help, it was written all over it. I gave the hairdresser a little smile and in a quiet voice, I told her to leave it to me. The tension on her face seemed to loosen. I had to take control of this situation and I knew something had to give, so I went in the room. Standing there was one brave woman hairdresser and Tanvi sitting in the chair. "It's not right," she bellowed, waving her hands about; Tanvi was stressed out. I needed to get her out of there for her own sake; stress was the last thing she needed in her condition. I quietly asked the hairdresser to leave, so she left. I gave Tanvi such a rollicking, asking her who she thought she was. I told her that it would never be perfect to her because it is not her hair, it's a wig, and she could either wear it or bin it. She sat there quietly. I continued to tell her that these women had worked hard to get everything right for her, and that she just could not see it as she was so wrapped up in herself. I instructed her that we were about to walk out of there, and if they smiled at her she would smile back. Tanvi started to relax; she seemed to come to terms with this not being her hair, and that it would never be the same.

The journey home was quiet, to say the least; I had not wanted to tell her off, but what was done was done, I had no choice. We got home and Mom naturally asked if everything was okay; I said yes and left it at that.

Later that day, I went upstairs to see if she was okay. Tanvi stuck her tongue out at me with a smirk on her face; she was fine. I went over, sat by her side and gave her a big hug, and naturally, she continued to complain about the wig while I held her, but this time it was more like a little child sulking than anything else. I apologised to her for the morning, she frowned at me in a childlike way and said I told her off. I told her she needed it, with a smile on my face. The wig would need maintenance but that's normal; they would wash it for her whenever. After that, her relationship with them was fine.

CONTINUAL TREATMENT

Tanvi's treatment would be every two weeks, with a meeting with the consultant on Thursdays at the Aspire Hospital in Little Aston. Consulting would always take place in the evenings around 19:30 every second week or on Tuesday evenings if we had to go to Solihull Parkway Hospital for some reason. This was due to the consultant working all day in the NHS and dealing with private patients in the evenings; that's a long day's work.

I found it highly stressful. My whole life would revolve around her treatment and evenings were spent looking after her, keeping the girls happy as much as possible and then I had work in the daytime. Going to work was a relief for me; it was my break from what was now my real job, nothing else really mattered. Even when I was at work my thoughts would be with Tanvi, thinking about the next treatment, making sure I had them all dated, what was going to happen and how would we get out of this. For the both of us there was no doubting that she would survive this; we had the Lord on our side, cancer treatment had advanced a lot over the years and we took encouragement from listening to other patients who had survived and were going strong, so why worry? The thought of Tanvi not surviving just didn't feature at all. We had it planned out: once she had had the mastectomy and radiotherapy, we would be in the clear; then all that would remain was the cosmetic surgery; after that, we'd be done. So we continued in a positive manner; everything was going to be fine.

OCTOBER 2012:
THE COKE BOTTLE
WAS ABOUT TO BURST

I had one major dependency in my life by now, someone who I would share with and who understood my situation. Sandra was going through her own trials at the time, her father was suffering from Alzheimer's disease and her walk was not easy. I would watch as Sandra mixed work with looking after her dad, creating a rota with her family members; however, the pressure was there for all to see, I could see it on her face. She didn't seem to reduce her workload, as far as I knew, and I suppose this was her way of coping with the situation. Sandra's experience with cancer was all too invaluable for me, as we went on our walks or if we had errands to run during lunchtime, I would accompany her or vice versa; we didn't necessarily talk about our issues all the time but we were able to just release some pressure. It was great therapy for me having someone to share with. It was when I had time to think and reflect on the situation. It was during those times of silence that I felt the pressure build up in me with a thousand and one thoughts running through my head, but it was okay because Sandra was there; I was covered.

However, Sandra was not always going to be there, as she went on leave for two weeks. Now I had no outlet and the consequences of that were about to hit the proverbial fan. Sandra's father was deteriorating; he needed to go into a home so he could be properly looked after. The pressure at home was too great, Sandra and her family needed help, so Sandra was off. I didn't notice at first, but when I found out Sandra was off, I was concerned, but I did nothing about it, I just carried on. Days would go past and I could feel the pressure building and building; I would pace around the office at times, looking for someone who would understand how I was feeling. However, they didn't have the experience that Sandra had, they didn't know how I felt and I wouldn't tell them as I wanted them to figure it out for themselves; Sandra could, so why couldn't they? I have the tendency to put on a face that says 'I'm okay', a mask of sorts; this mask came in the form of humour. Let's face it: no one can tell if you're hurting if you just laugh everything off. While this was going on, anger was building up in me all the time; on the inside I was hurting, on the outside the mask was in full cover-up mode. I was thinking, *Look, I'm laughing with you but I'm dying on the inside, can't you see that?* I just didn't get why they couldn't see it; Sandra would have picked it up in an instant, so they should have been able to. Sandra was the bar by which I examined everyone at the time and I was oblivious to what I was doing.

It all came to a head on the first Friday of September 2012; why do I remember this date? Because we have our team meetings on this day. So on this day I was ready to pop, you just say something wrong and I'm going to tear someone's head off. I was itching for a fight, it wouldn't have been physical, I'd have got the sack, but verbally, I was ready. Yet I was in enough control to ensure I wasn't booted out. Unfortunately, my Team Leader, Kiran, stepped up to the plate. This guy has taken a lot from me and I don't know what it is, personality clash or what, he's a good bloke and has been very supportive throughout. I just don't know, it's probably me. I don't even remember what the issue was but I know I just flipped. I was fuming when I went back to my desk. Kiran didn't even say anything, he just took it, which made me feel even worse.

I was shaken. I realised this was wrong, I needed to speak to my Line Manager, Steve Oliver, but we were about to have our Team Meeting so I waited until after the meeting. Kiran was cool as a cucumber; I think he realised something was up so he just took it. Mike Swales ran the meeting. I have no idea what he said in the meeting or what it was about, I was trying to keep it together, it was just background noise. Finally, the meeting was over. Steve did notice the flare-up in the office, and it's an open plan office: hard to miss someone having a tantrum.

We sat down and Steve spoke first. He said I was very good at putting on a face, making people think that everything was okay, but I wasn't, was I? I broke down, tears running down my face with my head in my hands; finally, someone could see what was going on. The whole situation was killing me, why us? Why her? Show me how to get through this, as I don't know how, what am I supposed to do? How do I stay strong

34

for her when I'm falling apart myself? How are the girls going to cope if I'm not strong enough?

Steve suggested counselling. I thought to myself, *Why do I need counselling? I don't need counselling.* It's amazing how, even through all this, we men can still make out as if we can just handle everything and anything, this 'macho man' mentality. To me, the very thought of counselling was a sign of failure. *It's only the weak that need counselling, I don't need counselling, I don't want counselling.* However, I don't think this was a suggestion from Steve. It was quite clear to him that I needed to do something. I couldn't carry on the way I was going.

Within Fujitsu, we have in place an employee assistance program (EAP). I had not really used it myself but I had suggested to former staff members that they use this system. But now, I had no choice; I had to do something and I just had that feeling of failure again. I was pretty down at this point, however, it had to be done, so I went down with Steve back to our office. Once at Steve's desk, he pulled out the EAP phone number and gave it to me.

Jim Higginson, who was the Account Director, came over to me and said "Let's go and have a chat." Jim was quite a lively character; you knew when Jim was in the office because you could hear him from afar. We went into a small room and Jim was very supportive. Jim had lost his mom to cancer after a long battle, so he understood. I wasn't dealing with someone here who had no experience in this area; Jim was very experienced. He talked about how his mother had fought hard against cancer but how she had passed away. I could see Jim's eyes filling up, yet he was willing to share with me. I was grateful for that; we spoke for a long time, and we must have been in there for at least forty-five minutes.

I was still not overly excited about having counselling, but I had no choice. I couldn't rely on Sandra all the time; frankly, it was not fair on her, she had enough of her own problems to deal with, without having to deal with mine. I wouldn't make that mistake again, relying too heavily on an individual who might be going through their own struggles and, frankly, who had no qualifications in this area, as I was to find out during my counselling sessions. Don't get me wrong; life experience is valuable, but these people are trained to deal with these kinds of situations, so they know what they are looking for.

Sometimes we talk about trusting in God, relying on him and the Lord to guide us through situations, but when you are facing immense pressure it is difficult. It's easy to quote Scripture when things are going well. We read the Bible and we start rolling off Scripture after Scripture as we give advice to people. However, when you go through stuff, and difficult times arrive, that's when your faith is tested; that's when you find out what the Scriptures really mean; are you going to turn away from him or are you going to run to him? Jesus didn't just quote Scripture, he crammed everything into a three and a half-year period where he was persecuted, ridiculed, and then crucified on the cross, and yet he said on the cross, "Father forgive them for they know not what they are doing," Luke 23 verse 34 NIV. I felt as if I was carrying my own cross and my cross was watching my wife go through treatment after treatment. I tell you now, it is only by the grace of God that I managed to get through everything, but not without scars.

I went home that evening and told Tanvi that I was going to have counselling. She looked at me sharply and said, "What for?" in a very negative tone. I said I needed help, I was struggling with a few things. I just needed to get them off my chest and if I didn't deal with this I was going to struggle.

I was feeling a bit better after letting off some steam, even if it was in the wrong manner; however, there was still a lot to get out. I just knew I wasn't quite right. I was unsure about many things; I wasn't confident and did not feel that I could handle the situation, or any, for that matter.

THE COUNSELLOR

A few days later I drove off to my first meeting with the counsellor. I specifically asked for a female counsellor; don't ask me why, I'm not sure myself. Maybe I just felt women make better counsellors. There is probably no basis for this view. However, my conversations with Sandra had been fruitful and I just felt comfortable speaking to a female counsellor. I arrived and was not sure what to expect; I had never been to counselling, and the counsellor seemed quite pleasant. We went into a small room and sat down. I was asked to sign the usual forms of confidentiality. She asked me how she could help; I told her about our situation and she listened intently.

I'm not sure what I expected. I told her everything about the cancer treatment; talking about it was difficult: I was shaken on the inside, and dealing with this was difficult. I was a bit irritated at first as I expected her to jump in and give me some answers but she just sat there listening, with that sympathetic counsellor's face she had. I can just hear her now: "So, how do you feel about my sympathetic counsellor's face?" "Annoyed," would be my answer to that. I wasn't looking for pity; I wanted answers. Tell me how to get out of this mess or, better, show me how to get through it, but don't just sit there nodding your head. An hour later, the session was finished, so we booked five more sessions. The hour wasn't a complete waste; I got to talk and let off some steam so I did feel better, however I still expected more. I left thinking, *Well, that wasn't much help.* My attitude to all this was very negative: I felt I was only having counselling because I was weak and I had failed.

The sessions took us into October and I will come back to them, however life had to go on. Kira was at the age where she had to pick her secondary school. Tanvi's treatment was now taking its toll, she was weaker and needed her rest, so it was my job to go round the schools in the evenings and inform Tanvi which school was the best. Tanvi was naturally upset that she couldn't go round the schools as this was a big thing for her, and also it was Kira – her firstborn, her baby.

There was one particular school we visited that didn't seem very happy to see the parents. This was due to her school and another clashing on dates. I believe the headmistress didn't like the idea of us going to her school second. She knew this was the case, hence, imagine a bunch of parents sitting in a hall with a grumpy looking woman who seemed to be telling us off. I glanced at Kira; she looked at me. She looked petrified, so we did the tour and left. I asked Kira, knowing what she was going to say, what she thought. "I'm not going to that school." I laughed and told her "Don't worry, I wouldn't go if I was you either." The school was good, however, it just didn't fit Kira's personality so we picked another school and Kira was happy. I did speak to the school and discussed Tanvi coming round later to check the school herself, and they were very helpful and welcoming on that matter. Kira was very excited about going to secondary school and was quite chatty to Tanvi about it all. I'm not sure how much Tanvi took in that evening, as she was feeling a bit tired.

TANVI'S FAMILY VISIT

Around October, we got word that Tanvi's aunt and mother were coming over to see her from India. They would spend a few months with us to help, and that was good. However, they were warned this was not the same Tanvi that they knew, she had no hair and was a lot weaker getting round the house as well.

They were due to come around the first week of December 2012, which irritated Tanvi because she had wanted them to come over before the mastectomy. Tanvi's irritation was down to the fact that she was very organised, someone who understood forward planning. They knew what the situation was and they knew that they would come over at some point. So why hadn't they got their passports ready in advance? Why was it that when it was time to go, they were only now starting to get all this ready? No one was going to get off lightly with Tanvi.

It was important for me that Tanvi wouldn't get so wound up or stressed out, so I would do my best to try and eliminate any potential areas of stress in her life. The private hospital was only allowed to ring me, any issues with bills or hospital appointments went through me. She was only allowed one visitor every two days; I was not prepared to move on this and didn't really care if a few people got upset; her well-being was my priority. Not many people knew she had cancer so that wasn't an issue at the beginning. The last thing Tanvi and I needed was people coming round with doom and gloom talk. I was in control mode; everything had to go through me, no questions asked. What was a plus was that we live in north Birmingham, right on the edge, bordering Walsall, so we never got that many visitors anyway. However, now that Tanvi's mom was coming, people were bound to ask why. Another bonus was, so was Tanvi's aunt, who, by this time, had visited eleven or twelve times; so as far as people were concerned, her mom was just tagging along.

MORE COUNSELLING
SESSIONS

I was on my third counselling session by now; I started to feel a lot more comfortable talking to the counsellor and started to open up more. During my second session, I did say to her that I didn't want to be there, but I had no choice. She understood, she understood about everything, which again I felt annoyed about. I'm not sure what I wanted, what I was expecting her to do or say. Tell me off, correct me or put me in my place, whatever, but stop agreeing with me. It was during the third session that I came to appreciate and respect the job she was doing. We were talking about a particular issue that had occurred in my early twenties and as I finished talking about it, she said, "We are finally getting to what is really bothering you."

I saw what she had done: she had guided me to a place where I would stop dancing around the issue and come to the point. I was impressed. I finally got what counselling was about. Up to then, I had been dancing around the real issues that were bothering me and it had taken me three sessions to get there. Her job was not to tell me what to do but to lead me to find the answers for myself. Counsellors are there to guide you, to help you to discover for yourself what the main issue is that is troubling you; it is up to you to deal with the issue; it's all about empowering you, the client. As I dealt with my problems, I felt a sense of relief. I was starting to gain control over our situation and myself; it was quite liberating. I would look forward to the remaining three sessions, taking note of what bothered me so I could address them each time. As each problem was addressed I felt stronger in myself, ready to tackle the issues of the day. I started with a very negative view of counselling – it was for wimps, people who could not handle things in life, the weak minded – and how wrong I was in my thinking.

We men sometimes have this great idea that we are all in control of everything that surrounds us. A lot of this probably rises from our upbringing: we live in a society where men are supposed to be men, strong, showing no weakness. I've recently been doing a course at Renewal called 'Knowing Me, Knowing You'. It's about how God sees us and we see ourselves. The last session dealt with how our environment affects us and how that environment fashions us into the people we are now, good or bad. During the period I grew up in, men were not supposed to show any feelings. I grew up in a house with a father who was strong. He was dominant, and everybody did what they were told, no questions asked. If you did ask, you were heading for trouble if it was a stupid question. I had this macho idea in my head and this was formed through my upbringing and what society expects from us. This is where all this nonsense came from in my head. I say it takes a real man to admit when he's weak and needs help and do something about it.

You shouldn't just sit there thinking that you can deal with every single issue that comes about, because you can't. My advice is, get help if you need to, no one needs to know. After my counselling sessions, I became a much stronger man and was able to deal with the difficult situations that were around the corner. The further six counselling sessions gave me a realisation that counselling was something that wasn't there to be ridiculed, but to be used to help you to come out of difficult situations. There is no shame in dealing with problems that are greater than you. My attitude changed dramatically. I'm the first now to advocate counselling for anyone who needs it, especially men, because let's face, it we are not very good at showing our emotions. We tend to hide things, we tend to think that we can deal with everything, but we can't, the mind is a lot more complicated than you might think. I finally had an outlet that didn't depend on others but a trained qualified counsellor. I had my friends; they would play a vital part in my life over the next few years, but I would think twice now about overburdening an individual who didn't have the qualifications and might be going through their own issues; that isn't right or fair.

Tanvi's treatment continued throughout October going into November. Every two weeks, we would go to see the consultant to discuss the latest progress. In the beginning, things seemed fine; the doctor was pleased the lump in her breast had started to shrink. We were pleased and we continued to pray. Prayer was a major part of our lives and would continue to be so; this wouldn't change even in our darkest times. The doctors were pleased that we were on schedule to go ahead and operate around the first week in December. However, when we got to the fourth meeting, the doctors were concerned that the lump in her breast had not shrunk but had remained stable. The cancer had already spread to the lymph nodes, checks had been done previously to ensure that it hadn't spread to the bones or any other part of the body. The very fact that the chemo was not having an effect on the lump concerned the consultant; it's normally expected that the lump would disappear completely. This happens in most patients who suffer from breast cancer; it's only a minority whose lump does not shrunk enough. So what did this mean? Those patients whose tumour cleared completely fell into the 80% survival rate, which is very good, along with the radiotherapy that would push them up to close to 95%. However, Tanvi fell into the 20% survival rate. Immediately, the doctors decided to bring forward the mastectomy. We had a window of opportunity; Tanvi would go into surgery within a week. Doctors were concerned that, if they didn't act immediately, things might deteriorate.

I don't know why, but that 20% survival rate didn't faze us; we were not overly concerned, or possibly it just didn't register mentally with us. As far as we were concerned, once she had the operation and all the affected lymph nodes were cleared and the breast was removed, the cancer would be gone, she would be cancer-free. That's the attitude we had and it stayed that way.

I was ready for this, my big hurdle. This is what had been concerning me from the beginning, but I was strong and mentally ready for this. I think we truly believed that, once the tumour and lymph nodes were removed, we would be fine. For those of you who are not sure what the lymph nodes are, we all have them; the best way I can describe them is that they are the junctions that lead to other parts of the body, a bit like our motorway junctions. The surgeon was very keen to make sure that all the lymph nodes affected were cleared; this, along with removing the breast, was a priority. Therefore, we went home and it was my job to tell everybody what was going to happen. Tanvi never dealt with these kinds of areas, they were my domain. Whatever the news, I had to deal with it, and I had to tell everybody who needed to know at the time.

When you go over the same topic repeatedly, it can drag you down. I used to wish that I could get all those who needed to know in one place and deal with it in one go; unfortunately, that's not the case. You go home and tell your parents, then you ring your brother, then you ring your sister and inform her, then I ring Tanvi's aunt in India, I would leave it to her to tell everybody else in India, those who knew. I would also ring my work colleagues, just my Team Leader, he would deal with telling whoever needed to know, and finally I would inform Tanvi's workplace. I think that covered everybody; every major piece of news, every bit of progress that was deemed important, that is what I would do. The girls were only told what they needed to know; our main aim here was to protect them; they were too young. There was only so much they could take. I did make it clear to the girls that Mommy would have to have her breast removed. Anjali was too young to grasp the situation

47

but Kira was old enough to understand what this meant. She really got upset and Tanvi would console her and tell her everything would be fine. Both girls would handle the situation differently; Anjali, being so young, would have her own way. She would leave little notes around the house for her mum to pick up saying, 'Get well soon Mom, hope you feel better.' Kira was all emotion. I could handle that, it was a lot easier to deal with someone who really did know how to cry and show his or her emotions. It's much more difficult for younger children to grasp what's going on. If I focused on the girls, that feeling of losing control would rise up in me. So I would block them out. It was important to me at the time that I remained strong to help Tanvi through surgery. I was not being mean; I just needed to focus.

DECEMBER 2012

The time had come for the day of the operation. We were ready for this, I was ready for this, in fact we wanted to get this done and out of the way. Having the operation out of the way, for us, was a sign that we were moving on. Once the breast was removed and the infected lymph nodes cleared out we would be okay, the cancer would be out of her body; so we looked forward to the operation. I'd had all the help that I needed, the counselling seemed to go well and I didn't seem to have any issues; Tanvi was ready as well, she was just as eager as I was so we could just get on with our lives. In our eagerness to move on, Tanvi and I decided that we would go on holiday; we decided we were going to enjoy ourselves and we decided to go on a Caribbean cruise. The best time to go on these cruises was around Christmas so we planned one for Christmas 2013, as the weather is perfect around the Caribbean during this time. We had plenty of leave between the both of us and we had a window of opportunity for the girl's school as well. We planned a fourteen-day trip around the East Caribbean and West Caribbean covering most of the major islands. We would fly over to Fort Lauderdale and then from there we would catch the cruiser. We decided to ask Mom and Dad to see if they wanted to come along.

Mom and Dad had already planned a trip to the Caribbean cruise a few years earlier but unfortunately, just before they were about to fly off, my dad suffered a heart attack. I remember that day, Dad sitting on the hospital bed asking the consultant, "What about my cruise?" The consultant replied, "This is your cruise." So we thought, wouldn't it be nice if they could finally get to go along, and we'd never been on holiday abroad with Mom and Dad. We had been to the Lake District together before, but never abroad. Yes, we had been to India, but I have never really classed India as a holiday. So off I went down the travel agents. I sat down and worked out an itinerary, took Dad with me, and we paid the deposit. We thought to ourselves, *Why not?* Once the mastectomy had been done and she'd had the radiotherapy, we could move on with our lives. It would then just be a case of planning the cosmetic surgery and the best time to have it done.

Getting back to the surgery, Tanvi was prepped and briefed, and the operation was to take place in the morning. My brother came along to support me, which was good. We were told that the surgery would take a good few hours so it made sense that we went home, considering home was only eight minutes away. As soon as Tanvi was out of surgery, the hospital would inform us and we would be there in the room to greet her. Even though I was at home, mentally I was with her. My brother did his best to keep me occupied, to no avail, and my thoughts were with her and nothing else. She came out of surgery and she was heavily sedated. I had a quick intimate moment with her just holding her hand, but did not dwell too much. I didn't want to risk getting over-emotional at this point, so I bottled it all in. I waited for the surgeon to give us a report on the operation; we had been informed, before Tanvi went in for surgery, that he would give a full account of how the operation went. About twenty minutes later, the surgeon came in and he was really happy with the operation. He felt that he had cleared out all the lymph nodes that were affected, I think he counted around thirteen to fourteen different lymph nodes that had been affected.

That was good to hear; it is what we wanted to hear, some good news at last. Finally, Tanvi would been cleared of these cancerous cells; it was now just a case of recovery. The lymph nodes help regulate the flow of water throughout the body, so having lymph nodes removed from under the arm and around the breast runs the risk of lymphoma. Lymphoma is where water can potentially build up in the arm around where the nodes had been removed, so Tanvi was given exercises to do to prevent this. The effect of water building up in the arm is not a pretty sight. I have seen this in other people, your hand can swell up around two to three times the thickness, and it is then much more difficult to deal with.

The surgery was the beginning of a journey of treatment; she still had radiotherapy to go through, but that would be after Christmas and we would enter January 2013 before the radiotherapy started.

Tanvi started to wake up from her operation. I informed her that the surgery went well and that the doctor was very pleased with the work that he had done. Tanvi gave me a faint smile, I smiled back at her. Tanvi would spend a few days in hospital and then it would be time to come home. It wouldn't be easy. Tanvi would have a bottle by her left side with a tube coming out of her ribcage, roughly four inches below her armpit, to allow fluids that would build up around the breast area to come out. Where once there was a breast, was now just a flat area. It was awkward for her and she would have to carry this bottle around for at least a week after we got home until the doctor was happy that the fluids were drawn out.

A few days later, we went home. Tanvi was carefully holding the bottle, and the tube was quite long and awkward so it was important we were careful of her movements. One of the staff members came with a wheelchair and wheeled her to the car, helping her gently into the vehicle. I told her not to rush and take her time, especially when getting out of the car, especially with this long tube sticking out of the side. As we got home, I told Tanvi to wait in the car while I came around to open the door for her. However, Tanvi was not known for her patience and she opened the door and tried to get out, catching the tube on the handbrake. Tanvi felt a tug and she winced. I wasn't best pleased; I told her if she had just listened for once it would actually help. She looked at me with a concerned look on her face, she was worried that she may have tugged the tube out. It was still in, so we went in the house and went upstairs and checked.

Everything was fine. I insisted that next time she was to wait for me and not get so impatient to move about because she can't right now, she was just going to have to go slow. The girls came home from school and gently gave Mom a hug.

That night, around one o'clock in the morning, Tanvi wasn't happy about the tube in her side; she felt as if it wasn't working properly. The bottle had the ability to draw out the fluid and as the bottle filled, she was to empty it out. If I recall, she was adamant the fluid wasn't coming out, so I rang the private hospital and they asked us to come in. I took her into the hospital and the doctor who was on call that night examined her. He stated that the tube was fine and everything was working well. I informed them that she had caught it on the handbrake and that she felt that it was loose in some way; the doctor reassured her that it was fine. I knew it was fine but it was no good coming from me, she had to have the doctor's opinion. We went home and finally got back to bed at two o'clock in the morning.

Tanvi was very fussy about who could examine her. I remember one night, during our many nightly trips to the hospital, we went to see the doctor and Tanvi was convinced that the doctor didn't have a clue what to do. The poor doctor was young and when the doctor went for advice I would get the full-on lecture about how the doctor kept second-guessing what was wrong and contradicting herself. All I could do was to keep Tanvi as calm as possible and reassure her the doctor knew what she was doing. Tanvi had a sharp mind, and this mind went to law school, so you can imagine she was very meticulous when it came to finding flaws in people's arguments. There was one particular doctor on call she was happy with. He was from Poland and in Poland he was a leading surgeon. Well, that just ticked all her boxes. Tanvi would make sure what type of doctor she was dealing with, they would get their own examination from her. "What was your previous role? Your position?" etc. I wasn't about to stop her; I got my head chewed off most days so let someone else have their turn. *Rather you than me,* I thought.

I made quite a few late-night trips to hospitals and pharmacies, with or without Tanvi, sometimes twice in a night, returning home late in the morning. If she didn't feel right or she needed some medication, I would make the run. The day trips were okay, however, most of the time the runs happened during the night. I would consult the nurses who were looking after Tanvi over the phone, and I had both their numbers in my phone so I had direct contact with them if needed. They were brilliant, willing to take my questions at ungodly hours. I moaned at Tanvi once, "Why can't you have an issue in the daytime? You always send me out at ridiculous times in the night." I still went, but I had to get that off my chest.

It was a difficult transition for Tanvi, having to walk around the house with a bottle by her side, trying to be careful not to catch the tube. I thought it best if she just sat in one place, which she did for most of the time. Tanvi was always a difficult person in that area, wouldn't sit still for one minute, which made life a bit more difficult for all of us. However, as the days went on, she managed to adjust and we developed a routine to help her empty the bottle out. That week we would have regular check-ups to make sure everything was fine; this was part of her scheduled checks and not one of her unscheduled checks, I hasten to add.

It was a week later that the bottle finally came off which was a lot better for Tanvi, and for my nerves as well. Once the bottle was gone it gave her the flexibility to move around the house, but she was still very sore and she had a massive bandage over the left side of her chest. By now, Tanvi was wearing a prosthetic bra, but this was only after the wound had healed up enough so when she put the bra on it wouldn't cause any discomfort. You couldn't tell, to be honest; once the bra was on she looked fine, so it was easy to forget that it was not real. But at night when she would get undressed, that was when you were back to reality.

Once again, Tanvi had one of those nights where she felt the wound wasn't healing well. I told her it looked fine, but she was adamant that she wanted to get it checked out so once again we went off around midnight to the hospital to get the wound checked. It was only a ten minute drive to the hospital, so that was a blessing. On the way there Tanvi would wind herself up by hoping the good doctor was there, so I tended to learn to just switch off at times, much to her annoyance. During all these hospital visits and appointments, you are fed a lot of information and it was quite clear that Tanvi was not going to take all this information in. Therefore, it was up to me to listen to what the doctors would say. It was important that I understood as much as possible, especially when they talked about the wound and how it should heal and how it should look. The wound was difficult to look at; there were stitches coming from the centre of her chest right across to just under her armpit. By now, you could start to see her ribcage as the skin naturally tightened around the area. I took her to see the doctor that night and the doctor examined the wound. I also described to him what I expected to see, according to what the surgeon had told us. He agreed the wound looked fine, there wasn't anything really wrong; it was healing nicely. Tanvi was just concerned and frustrated really, but it was important for her own peace of mind that there was no potential infection in the wound. Not only her physical well-being was important to me, but also her state of mind.

Our chemo consultant told us that how the patient deals with the illness in is the mind, and how positive they remain has a major impact on their survival rate. I could relate to this. When you're down and feeling low you tend to start aching in the body. This was so true in my case; back pain, neck pain, mainly due to the high levels of stress you tend to endure during difficult times.

Therefore, while I knew the wound was fine according to what I had learnt, we still went to the doctor's, letting the experts tell her that it was fine. I was happy with that, as long as she was happy and at peace with her situation, and let's face it, nothing is more reassuring than a doctor telling you that it's okay.

We did have our funny moments that night. I have always been the type of person who was confident in what I was saying or doing, whether I was sure it was the right thing to do or the right path to take, it didn't matter; I say, make a decision and stick to it. I knew what the surgeon had told me, so as I spoke with the doctor on call that night I did it with confidence; I was just repeating what we had been told. I knew what the wound should look like. However, much to Tanvi's annoyance, as we were leaving, the nurse asked me if I was a doctor. Tanvi groaned, this had happened to me before on a number of occasions in hospitals. I don't know what it is, I suppose if you walk around in a long coat in a hospital, look confident, walk with a purpose, people might actually think you're a person of importance, even a doctor. Let's face it, we see a lot of Asian doctors around hospitals so I qualified in that area. A Dr Naik works out of Good Hope Hospital so with my surname being Naik, some people just put two and two together and got five. I would look at Tanvi with a smile on my face whenever someone mistook me for a doctor. I would joke with her that she was in safe hands, Dr Naik was on the case. She would roll her eyes at me mumbling to herself while I would walk out with a smug look on my face. I think we got home at one o'clock that night; that wasn't so bad.

NEGATIVE REACTIONS

I remember that before Tanvi went to the physiotherapist, she had already been given some basic massages by the nurse and instructions from the doctor on how she must stretch that area where the left breast used to be and the upper arm area. One night Tanvi said she was fed up doing them and she asked me if I could do them. As she stood in front of me with her open wound, my first reaction was a negative one. I almost took a step back immediately, for at that instant, the thought of touching that area repelled me. Then I realised how hurtful my reaction must have been to her. I was disgusted with my reaction; I had seen the wound repeatedly but I had never touched the wound or that area. Tanvi said "It's okay, I'll do it." However, it was too late; the damage was done. If Tanvi was hurt by my reaction, she never let me know; there was no sign of disappointment on her face.

I went into work the next day feeling down, full of guilt and disappointed with my reaction. I was supposed to be her husband and yet I had reacted in a negative way. I was upset with myself. I didn't tell anybody about what I had done, I was too ashamed of myself, but I was determined that, when I went home, I would man up. That night I said to her, "I'll do that," and started to massage across the wound up towards the shoulder. I was okay after that and she was a lot more pleased. I told her that I hadn't been happy about the way I reacted last night, and I let her down, but she seemed fine about it. I never could understand Tanvi at times, the things I expected her to get upset about, she wouldn't, and the things that I didn't expect her to get upset about, she would; I don't think I have ever understood that about her. Tanvi was diligent with her exercises and we would do them together.

A TRIP TO THE AIRPORT

The time had come for the arrival of Tanvi's aunt and mother from India. To make life easier for me, Tanvi's aunt had decided to book a flight into Birmingham Airport. Previously, I had travelled down to Heathrow Airport, and I wasn't very keen on being too far away from Tanvi, just in case she needed some help. The flight was in the evening so they would arrive at Birmingham Airport around 6:30pm. I remember picking them up that day and discussing with them on the way home Tanvi's condition; she was in good spirits but she wasn't the same person they last met. She had no hair, she had no left breast and she would move around the house a lot slower. However, I told them not to expect her mental capacity to be any slower, she was as sharp as ever. It was an emotional meeting for them both. I felt for her mother, I can't imagine having to deal with your child who is ill from a long distance. They soon adjusted to life here; their arrival relieved a lot of pressure off my mom who was taking up a lot of the burden in the house. When Tanvi was not able to get around the house, my mom would deal with all the cooking.

Mom was seventy-five with a bad knee and it was difficult to see her having to deal with this situation at her age; so now, at least, she would have some help in the household. Tanvi's aunt stayed until just after Christmas, and her mother stayed on a lot longer, into the New Year.

As the weeks went on, Tanvi's wound healed up quite nicely. Her radiotherapy wasn't planned until the New Year 2013, so she had a nice break over the Christmas period. I decided that I wanted to do something nice for her that Christmas and was determined to buy her something. Therefore, I went into work to get some ideas. I'm not the best at doing something romantic or with great affection; whenever I would try, I never could quite get it right. I asked around in the office for ideas; money wasn't an issue on this occasion. I just wanted to spoil her a bit. One of my work colleagues and friends, Davinder Birring (Dav), was good at this kind of stuff. He suggested creating a basket of things, which I thought was a great idea, so one lunchtime we went out in Telford and with his help created a wonderful basket of perfumes, chocolate and other stuff I can't remember, but it was all decorated nicely. Dav was great and it seemed so easy for him to do; this is the type of person I worked with, who were fantastic during difficult times.

Dav was and is a funny man, full of quick one-liners, and always had a way of making me laugh. During difficult times, being able to laugh was like finding gold; there were times when I would drive to work hoping that Dav would make me laugh and forget our situation, and true to character, he would. If you ask Dav now what he did to help during these times, he would say, "Nothing". But I tell you the truth, his ability to add humour during a difficult time was invaluable. These were desperate and dark times, and anything to break the cycle of constantly thinking of treatment after treatment was welcomed; Dav played his part and a crucial part it was; I salute you, my friend.

We looked forward to Christmas; it was a welcome break from treatment after treatment. It was our turn to host Christmas day and it was probably the right thing to do as I didn't want Tanvi out in the cold or running the risk of catching an infection. Christmas day was fun, especially as I had my gift for her under the tree. I felt like a little child waiting for someone to open their gift, thinking, *Open it! Open it!* waiting for that approval of satisfaction. She opened it with a big smile on her face; it was so pleasing to see. I think I was more excited than she was, I had to control my enthusiasm and I think I took more pleasure out of it than she did. Over Christmas, we tended to play games all day and eat all day as well, with a few good drinks to wash it all down. Tanvi wasn't allowed to drink if I recall, due to the chemo treatment she had; she was not pleased, as she liked a glass of red wine or two.

We were coming to the end of December and Tanvi was given the task of examining the wound and the surrounding area during this period; this was to ensure that, if she felt something out of the ordinary, the chemo consultant needed to know. One night, Tanvi said to me that she felt a lump under her collarbone that had not been there before, so I checked, hoping really that it was just in her mind. However, she was right, so we rang the hospital and they confirmed through tests that both lumps were cancerous.

This was the first time I was concerned. Tanvi had now had over six sessions of chemo and a mastectomy, all that was left was the radiotherapy. I felt the radiotherapy was the last line of defence; I thought, *What if that didn't work, then what?* It was agreed by the consultant that the radiotherapy machine would be realigned to cover this area. The radiotherapy machine is a sophisticated piece of equipment. To ensure this was done accurately, Tanvi would have I think three to four laser marked points surrounding the area that was to be treated. These marks or black dots were burnt onto her skin, a permanent imprint if you will. This allowed the machine to be precisely placed each time to cover the area concerned. The treatment would only last a couple of minutes, due to the levels of radiation we were dealing with. After the new lumps were found, her treatment was increased to the maximum possible, twenty days in a row. What radiotherapy does is destroy all living cells in that area so nothing would grow in that area again. I always compared it to a last resort treatment, a nuclear bomb to cover the area, to ensure we got this finally.

The effects of radiotherapy on the skin are quite horrendous. By the end of the treatment, Tanvi's left shoulder area and left chest area looked like she'd been scalded with boiling hot water; it was severely red and looked extremely painful. These were testing times for Tanvi. She went through terrible pain as they couldn't put a tight covering over the wound and it was open to the elements. Putting on clothing was a challenge and it was a two-man job, no way could she do it on her own. Tanvi was given the option of taking morphine to help with the pain, but she was more concerned with getting addicted to morphine. Her stubbornness would test my limits during this period. We tried all types of painkillers; the basic over-the-counter drugs were just too weak, so they gave her codeine, but that gave her constipation, which didn't help at all. One drug after another we tried, but to no avail. I told her straight off that I was going to get the morphine and that she was going to take it, whether she liked it or not, no questions asked. So I picked up the morphine and she took it; this seemed to work but she reacted badly to the morphine as well. Now she was completely flat out in bed; that made me feel even worse as I had just contributed to her agony. During this period I was off work, and I was stressed out completely. Tanvi was groaning to me to do something; she could hardly speak, moving her head side to side in bed. She would finally fall asleep late into the night, sometimes around 3 o'clock in the morning. I kept monitoring her temperature to ensure that she was fine. It was important for Tanvi to avoid a high temperature, as this was possibly a sign that she may have an infection. Her blood T-cell count was important: if it dropped too low that could spell danger, she could slip away; thankfully, her temperature was normal. This went on night after night and it was a week later that Tanvi started to feel better. The girls would pop in every now and then, to check how Mom was doing. Kira was visibly upset, you could tell. The strain of the last week told on us all. The good thing was, she had started to feel better; this was evident when Tanvi in her indelible way decided to have a pop at me for making her take the morphine, and she was not pleased. I've never known someone to have such a delicate stomach that she would react to any form of medication. Okay, morphine is heavy, I understood that, but the only thing she didn't react to was paracetamol, and that was useless in this situation. I was told that under no circumstances would she be taking morphine again; I didn't really argue with her on that point. I would stress that each medication was taken under the observation of the doctors at the hospital as they were always on the other end of the phone. It was not as if I was pumping her with drugs to calm her down; however, at times, it felt like a good idea.

Tanvi was booked in to receive some physiotherapy; this was to stop the muscles and the skin tightening over the wound, so she would maintain some flexibility in her hand and maintain a range of movements. The physio was set up at Little Aston Hospital. She went to the first session on her own as she said she didn't need me there. However, I was asked to come to the next one by the physiotherapist to help in performing some basic massages. So every week she would go for her physiotherapy and I would go with her, when asked to do so. They would teach me new techniques in massaging to help her in her recovery.

2013

We now entered the New Year and throughout January her radiotherapy continued. We resigned ourselves to the knowledge that the treatment needed to be extended and that a new lump had been found and it had to be dealt with; however, all seemed well and we were both optimistic going into this year. Tanvi's year started with the following programme:

Friday 4th Jan – Chemotherapy
Monday 7th to Friday 11th Jan – Radiotherapy
Monday 14th to Friday 18th Jan – Radiotherapy
Monday 21st to Friday 25th Jan – Radiotherapy
Monday 28th Jan to Friday 1st Feb – Radiotherapy
Monday 4th Feb – Chemotherapy

After this, she needed a CT scan and then a bone scan, and then Tanvi would not be seen again by the consultant for at least another six weeks, then visits to the consultant every three months.

The strain of the radiotherapy did take its toll on me and I arranged for some more counselling for myself. I suggested to Tanvi that she ought to have counselling, but she refused; it was her choice but later on in the year, she would eventually change her mind.

Tanvi's hair was growing back nicely, she was also massaging oil into her head to ensure her hair would grow back evenly. Tanvi was clued up in all these things; she would still continue to wear the wig well into the year. Things were looking up, we both felt that we were now coming out the other end and we could start to move on in our lives. Cancer can bring your life to a sudden stop; it's like playing a board game when you have to miss a turn. You feel as if everyone is moving on but you haven't or you can't; that's how it felt for us. For the first time in a while, we started to plan for the future. We were always told by the doctors that Tanvi would have to go two years clear without incident for her chances of survival to increase, so that was always in the back of my mind and I'm sure this was in her mind as well. However, we thanked the Lord for where we were and were grateful that we could now move on in life.

FEBRUARY 2013 –
PLANNING
COSMETIC SURGERY

We were now into February, her healing was coming on nicely and Tanvi was already planning to have cosmetic surgery to restore her left breast. We discussed this and, frankly, we had a few disagreements in this area as to the timing. It was quite clear Tanvi was mindful of the coming cruise we had planned for the end of 2013, and wanted to look her best. She was also fed up with the false implant in her mastectomy bra (mastectomy bras are available for purchase allowing you to place an implant in the cup). So we discussed the timing with the consultant. I was more cautious and agreed with the consultant that it would be best that she had the surgery well into 2014; the reason for this was if she had the surgery three to six months after the radiotherapy and it came back, they would have to tear down all the work that the cosmetic surgeon had done. Tanvi wanted it done around September 2013, before the cruise. I thought this was such a tight margin of recovery before December, and we were due to fly out on the 21st December. It took a while, and I got a bit of an earful, but the doctor and I prevailed and she agreed to wait until 2014. However, nothing comes easy with Tanvi; she still wanted to go and visit the cosmetic surgeon to start the prep work and the selection of what she wanted.

THOSE LIGHTER MOMENTS

I remember one day walking into a conversation Tanvi was having with my sister on the phone, about what is now called 'the boob job'. Tanvi was joking about going a few cup sizes bigger, D+, and considering she was five foot three and petite I told her she would most likely fall over due to balance issues. I remember saying to her, "I don't think so," and she laughed, however she was planning to go to a D from a C. I was unsure and I asked her whether she had considered that she might have to change her wardrobe. Now I had caught her attention; her second biggest interest in her life: her clothing. My motives were purely self-serving, to stop her from going to a larger cup size; that backfired on me. Tanvi always dressed well, even if she was going to work. For me, work is work, you just put something on and go, but for Tanvi it was a fashion statement. She would pull out clothes the night before and ask if this or that was appropriate. I would suggest, "Why don't you just get a set of clothes for work and wear those?" This was greeted with a comment of how useless I was, resulting in me being totally ignored as she went through her stuff.

Tanvi was now concerned. What if she had to change all her clothes? What if nothing fitted if she went to a bigger size? (A pointer here: when they perform the surgery they don't just do the one side, they do both, for obvious reasons.) I was now concerned about the cost of replacing all her clothes. I suggested she stick to her current size; however, she was not best pleased with that idea. Therefore, as a joke I suggested that she go into a few stores and take some tissues with her, try a couple of dresses and see if they fit. I said it AS A JOKE! She said, "Okay, this weekend we are going." I couldn't believe what I was hearing. This was ridiculous; I told her I'd been only joking. She said it made sense. I argued, "Since when did I start making sense?" She was adamant this was what we were going to do. The girls found out we were going into town. They wanted to come, but I said "No," in a sharp tone, which caused a tantrum. Tanvi explained to them that we would be back soon. Kira wanted to know why we were going; I think Tanvi sorted that out and made some excuse.

Therefore, Saturday turned up and off we went into Walsall shopping centre. Frankly, this was all a bit silly. Tanvi kept going on about how she didn't want to change her wardrobe and how she had some dresses she could not replace, while I kept mentioning the cost of it all. I was stuck in two minds; if this worked, she stayed the same size and I would save money on clothes; if it didn't, the question was, would she be willing to change her wardrobe? To be honest, I had no say in the matter. We finally arrived at a major store and went straight to the women's section; a female staff member came over and asked me if she could help. Now picture the scene: I am going through women's bras looking at labels for sizes; this did not look good at all. Tanvi came over and asked if I had found one yet. At that point, the staff member realised I was looking at bras for Tanvi and not for some other mischievous venture; she walked away. What she was thinking, God only knows. I said that, yes, I had found one, so off she went into the changing rooms. Ten minutes later, she came out looking very curvy. She immediately asked what I thought, and I told her to turn around and inspected the back. The dress seemed to fit perfectly; in fact, where it might have been a bit loose before at the back, as she was so petite, the dress fitted just right. She was most pleased, mission accomplished. Tanvi was most happy that she wouldn't have to change her dresses and she had made her mind up about what size she was going to go to.

I told her to go and get changed, but she had one more dress to try on. I said that's fine but I didn't need to see it, so if she was happy, she should just come out with her normal clothes and then we could go, as I wasn't fond of hanging around the ladies' section. I figured that was the end of that, we had already decided that she would have the surgery in the new year, all things being well, so what was the rush? Tanvi had other ideas. Tanvi was not content on just trying on the dress armed with tissues; now she wanted to arrange a meeting with the cosmetic surgeon for an initial discussion. There is one thing you need to understand about Tanvi: once she made up her mind, that was it. Once she had that steely, determined look on her face, she was going to go ahead whether you liked it or not, so an appointment was arranged for June 2013.

THE PARIS TRIP

Things were looking up and we were coming up to our fifteenth wedding anniversary. Since the girls had been born, the only time we had had a break on our own was on our tenth wedding anniversary, and that was to London for the weekend. That weekend, we had been to see a play in Leicester Square and had spent the night in Leicester Square. That trip was enjoyable so I wanted to do something special, something that did not involve the girls. I put it to Tanvi and her first reaction was, "What about the girls?" I said, "No girls, just you and me for the weekend."

She finally relented and agreed so I arranged a long weekend in Paris. We would fly out on the 19th April and would be back home on the 21st April; our anniversary was on the 20th April, so it was perfect. We told the girls what we were planning... well, sort of... we told them we were going to London; if we had told them we were going to Paris, they would have complained like mad. Anjali's first reaction was, "Great, where are we going?" I said, "Not we, just us." Kira immediately claimed that it was not fair; her first reaction is always emotional, then she will think about it. I informed them that, as we look after them 364 days a year, I was sure they could spare us for a weekend. I knew that if we told them where we were going they would want to come along, but I was adamant it was going to be just us two. Tanvi would sulk a bit about the girls not coming, like someone who had just lost their puppy, but I was determined; I wanted a break with just the two of us. We were going to do a family holiday in the summer anyway, so no, this was our turn. So Paris it was and we had a fantastic time; I made sure we stayed close to the sights, so we did not have far to travel. I still had to make sure that Tanvi was strong enough and we did the full tour on the bus around the city. For both of us, it was the best time we ever had; Paris was such a beautiful place and, yes, very romantic. The trip was so good we decided that from now on every year we would do a mini-trip on our own; we deserved that after all the treatment and stress. Things were going to be different; we would enjoy our lives instead of always worrying about the future, sometimes you have to live in the now and enjoy yourselves. To those of you who have partners, do not wait for things to happen, do not put things off, do it now if you can and spend time together. Enjoy the moment, life is too short; trust me, I know.

GETTING BACK TO WORK

As the weeks went by, we started to think further ahead about our future and what we would do. I started to ponder other jobs within the company to see what else I could do. It was important that I did this, as I needed to take some of the pressure off Tanvi. While I had a good job, Tanvi's job paid better and she would soon surpass me when it came to wages. There was potential for moving; however, a lot depended on management decisions within other departments for me to move on, so it was a waiting game.

Moving on to a new role was always a plan I had in my mind but with the cancer and ensuring Tanvi was looked after, everything else was put on the back burner. However, as I said, things were looking good.

THE WIG

We were well into May, moving into June. As I recall, Tanvi's hair was growing really well, she was now getting to a stage where she really didn't need to use her wig; however, this was a choice that she had to make on her own. As long as she felt comfortable without wearing the wig then I was happy. I thought she looked great without the wig; regarding hairstyles, it didn't matter whether she had long hair or short hair, I thought she looked great, and so did others. This wasn't a case of me just saying something to support my wife; let's face it, my opinion was always going to be favourable anyway; however, others said the same. Tanvi eventually decided to drop the wig; it was not easy putting the wig on, it was fastened with double-sided sticky tape on the inside along the edge, keeping it firmly in position. Underneath that, Tanvi's own hair was growing. It's difficult to get an idea of how it felt to wear a wig, let alone on top of your own hair that is growing. A few weeks went by and the wig was just sitting there in the room. Tanvi had lost interest in grooming it, so it was okay if I examined it a lot closer.

One Saturday morning I got up late. Tanvi was already downstairs and so were the girls. I spotted the wig in the corner and I was curious to try it on; I made my way to the dressing table where it sat. I picked it up and proceeded to place it on my head. I could not believe the weight of this wig; it was heavy, almost like wearing a helmet. I only put it on for a couple of minutes and I was amazed. How she wore this day to day was beyond me; it was difficult to move my head around and yet she did it with such ease. Suddenly I heard footsteps coming up the stairs. Tanvi came into the room and as I turned around she burst into laughter, asking what I was doing. I told her it looked good on me. While laughing she said, "You're an idiot, take it off." At this point, Kira walked into the bedroom. I started to swagger across the room with the wig on, and Kira hit the floor. I have never seen anyone laugh so much, she couldn't speak she was too busy rolling around the bedroom floor, while Tanvi continued her demands, telling me to take off the wig while shouting, "You idiot." Anjali was sitting on the toilet so I decided to pay her a visit. I walked in, she looked up and screamed loudly, she took a closer look and shouted, "Dad, take it off, that's scary." There was no stopping me now, I was in full flow prancing around the bedroom with this ridiculous wig on; bear in mind I had not had a shave for a day and a half so I looked quite hideous. Tanvi left the room still chuckling, telling me to take it off and reminding me how stupid I was. I finally took the wig off, which stopped Kira from rolling around on the floor. She commented, "Don't ever do that again," with a big smile on her face. My head was sweating after just wearing that wig for a short period of time; how she wore it day in day out is beyond me, it felt so uncomfortable. I got a small glimpse of how it must've felt for her wearing the wig; it was never going to feel like her own hair, so I can understand her frustrations with the wig; sometimes we don't fully comprehend how it might feel for the other person. I was very self-conscious just for that short period so she must have felt that way all the time. I did discuss this with her and how she managed it. She said, "Now you know how I felt." To all of you women out there who are wearing these wigs, I commend you for actually wearing them, and partners: learn to be a bit more sympathetic as our hair is not as important to us as it may be to your partner.

JUNE 2013 –
MEETING WITH THE
COSMETIC SURGEON

The time had come to meet the cosmetic surgeon; she was a polite woman with an excellent reputation in the industry for outstanding work so we were in safe hands, as I had done my homework. Tanvi was going to have the surgery so there was no point in me being negative over the issue, so I was going to make sure that Tanvi had the right type of implants and I went armed with a load of questions. I knew the surgeon's name so I went online and investigated the type of work the surgeon had carried out. I was interested in the type and quality of the implants she had used on her previous patients. It was important for me to know how safe these implants were after hearing about all the horror stories from the past, and some of them quite ridiculous really. However, my stories were from the past so my information was based on old information and hearsay. I wanted to make sure, whatever Tanvi was going to have was the latest in terms of implants and that she would not suffer any difficulties in the future.

The meeting was going well, we sat down and I asked

questions regarding the implants and the best type that were available. I think the consultant was pleasantly surprised as she wasn't sure what kind of input I would have into this conversation. I was fully engaged in helping with this even though I thought it was a year too early, as the surgery would not be taking place for another year. I realised for Tanvi this was all about moving forward, this was a sign we were coming out of this difficult period and we were able to move on with our lives. Therefore, as long as she felt that this was all about progression, I was happy to go along, I was happy to take part. Therefore, we sat down and listened intently to the consultant. I was pleased with what I was hearing, so the time had come for Tanvi to be measured. While the consultant and Tanvi carried on talking, to my surprise, I was handed what looked like a family photo album and I was told by Tanvi that these were for me to look at. I was a bit confused, or a bit naïve; I opened the first page and the album was full of women who had previously had cosmetic surgery on their breasts. I sheepishly started flicking through the pages observing shoulder-down shots of women's breasts. I have to admit this was a bit awkward; here I was in a hospital flicking through an album looking at women's breasts. On any other given day that would have spelt trouble, so as a consummate professional I carried on flicking through the pages. At first I was not sure what I was supposed to be looking for, then I realised I had to try to find a shape that would suit Tanvi. Tanvi came over and asked, "Any luck"? I thought to myself, here I am sitting looking at women's breasts and she asks me, "Any luck?" I didn't know what to say at first so I said, you have a look and tell me what you think, and that seemed the easy way out. The consultant was still in the room; if it had just been Tanvi and me, I think it would have been a lot more comfortable. I probably would have cracked a few stupid jokes as well on the way and got in trouble for it, but hey, nothing new there.

After another ten or fifteen minutes, the meeting was over. Tanvi was satisfied that she had fulfilled everything she wanted to, it was another milestone we had crossed. As I stated previously this whole exercise for me was a bit too early as we were still in the early stages of her recovery; there was still a chance that the cancer could come back. However, what was important was how Tanvi felt and she was happy that we were moving forward; nothing was more important to me than ensuring that she was happy. Tanvi had been through a lot of mental stress, tension and worry; she ran the gauntlet of emotions so, if she was happy, I was happy. I'm sure she had the same concerns as me, that we were still in the early stages; maybe this was another form of her creating a distraction from the situation and of all that she had just been through. It didn't really matter; I was willing to go along with it.

JULY 2013

The holiday season was upon us; the girls had just broken up from school and we had planned a holiday to Spain for the four of us. The girls enjoy their waterparks so we made our way down to Salou in Spain. We stayed in a four-star hotel with a waterpark nearby. I have to say, it was extremely hot; the temperature was touching the forties on some days. We did a little sightseeing, which included a trip to Barcelona and a tour around the Camp Nou stadium, home of FC Barcelona, shopping and other activities.

However, just before we left, Tanvi developed a slight cold and cough. We thought nothing of it, normally once you enter warmer climates these things tend to burn away so we continued to enjoy our trip. We would split our days into two halves; the morning session we would spend at the waterpark, then after spending a good few hours there we would get back to the hotel so Tanvi could get some rest. Tanvi still needed her rest and the girls fully understood this. In the evening, we would walk across the beach with the girls, enjoying the scenery.

It was about halfway through the holiday that we noticed Tanvi's cough was not going away; the cold had gone but the cough was still there. We agreed once we got back we would get it checked out. However, this was not going to spoil our holiday and we continued to have fun.

AUGUST 2013 –
BACK HOME

After spending ten days in Spain we were back home. Tanvi was very vigilant when it came to checking for any lumps or abnormalities around her collarbone. Unfortunately, Tanvi found a lump again, but this time it was on the right side of the collarbone. I booked an appointment to see the consultant. On 8th August we went in and Tanvi was instructed to go and have a full scan on 9th, the next day. It was possible that, due to the cough she had developed, it may have been a reactive gland, or it could have been cancerous. The plus point was, it was on the other side. Tanvi could not have radiotherapy on the left side again, as she had had the full dosage already, and hence this could be treated with radiotherapy if needed.

HEARING THE
UNIMAGINABLE

The appointment was not until 15th August so we went about our daily routine. I was still looking to move on to pastures new and a potential opportunity came up which I was keen on. As far as we were concerned, things were still looking up. A week had gone by and it was time to see the consultant. Tanvi and I were a bit apprehensive yet prepared for her having to have some more radiotherapy if necessary. By now, we were good at reading the consultants' facial expressions as to the type of news we would get, but nothing prepared us for what we were about to be hit with.

We went in and sat down and his face looked serious. It was cancerous, however, the cough that Tanvi had developed was due to the cancer spreading to her chest wall. I asked him what did this mean? He said that, because it had spread to her chest wall, they could treat it but not cure it.

It did not make sense to me what he was saying. Tanvi looked at me in disbelief. I asked him what he meant by that. It just did not register with me; how can you treat something but not cure it? He said he was sorry. Reality sank in for Tanvi. She started sobbing loudly. I was shaking, with tears in my eyes. The ultimate question came into my mind:

How long has she got? I couldn't ask him in front of Tanvi; she still needed protecting.

By this time, the nurse had taken Tanvi and me into another room. Tanvi was uncontrollable at this point. I had a thousand questions going through my mind. Tanvi's pain was deep and heavy; the girls came into her mind and she kept repeating "What about my girls?" I fell to my knee by her feet and we just cried. I had no words for her; nothing I could say was going to help. It took all I had to compose myself. I focused on the only aspect of my life that gave us a glimmer of hope: my faith, my Lord Jesus Christ. I was totally broken. I started to hold her tight by the shoulders and told her to look at me, I told her we still have the Lord, and that we were going to lean on him fully and he would deliver us from this. It took a good fifteen minutes to get ourselves together. I still had a load of questions. At this point, the nurse came back in so I took the opportunity to go and see the consultant. I had to ask him how long she had. I really did not want to know, but I had no choice, so I went in and asked him the question. He said he didn't know at this point. Tanvi and I went back into the consultant's room, as we needed to know what next. Tanvi had calmed down and the consultant said because it had not spread to the lungs, he would do his best to supress it, keep it under control. The consultant told us he was surprised that she had gone six months clear; they had expected it to come back within three months.

The cancer that Tanvi had was an aggressive type, but there was no way we thought it would come to this. Our world had just been blown away, we were now faced with this massive mountain. This was way too big for us to deal with on our own, and we were going to need help. The consultant spoke to us regarding the type of treatment Tanvi could have. All the chemo she had previously had was no good, so Tanvi was given experimental chemo, which was not available on the NHS. If I had not had private cover, this would have not been available to her.

I knew now that all we had left was our faith in God, so as we went home that evening I reminded her that we needed to focus on trusting God and that by his grace that was the only avenue we had; we needed a miracle. Naturally we cancelled the cruise; we only lost the deposit but that was the last thing on my mind.

TELLING THE REST
OF THE FAMILY

I now had the difficult task of telling my parents the grim situation and most of all, how was I going to tell the girls? We both decided that we would not tell the girls anything straight away, there was no point; we had no idea how long Tanvi actually had so we thought it wise to carry on as best we could. Mom and Dad were devastated. Mom was asking "What about the girls?" It was hard to take, and thinking back now I don't know how we got through it all.

I rang India the next day and informed them. I spoke to her auntie, as I did not have the heart to tell her parents and brother; she passed on the news. My brother had come over and I spoke to him, he is normally made of sterner stuff, but even he buckled under this news.

Each time I told someone it was like placing a weight on my shoulder, my mind was once again fully loaded with one thought after another. I needed to be strong for her, but how? On the Monday I went into work. Tanvi and I decided that we would try to keep things as normal as possible. I remember the meeting I had with my Team Leaders and Operations Manager. There were long pauses of silence, as they just did not know what to say to me. Mali was in tears and I offered to get her some water. She said, "We should be consoling you." Mali had met Tanvi as her children and mine went to the same school, so naturally when you put a face to a name it is always going to be harder. Once again, the team was excellent, supporting me in every way they could. Regarding my career, this was no time to leave, so I emailed the manager to whom I was going to apply for a job and told him that I would not be moving. This was no time for change and frankly, stress levels had just been ramped up so it would not have been fair on the other team.

RENEWAL
CHRISTIAN CENTRE

That Friday or Saturday night, I cannot quite remember, Tanvi stated that we needed to go to church; it had been nearly two years since we entered a church we could call home. Tanvi asked me, "What about Renewal, you know some people there, why can't we go there?" Therefore, I got onto my Facebook and contacted one of my old friends, who attended Renewal.

I had long been friends with Julia and Cyrille Regis; going back to my old church, however, we had lost contact for a while and had only communicated via Facebook. Cyrille's name might ring a bell with keen footballers out there, as he used to play for West Bromwich Albion, Aston Villa, and Coventry City, to name a few clubs. That night I sent a private message to Julia regarding our situation and we agreed to go to Renewal the following Sunday. Cyrille met us and we were both impressed with the size and how vibrant the church was. We were introduced to a few other friends, Bryan and Jan Hewitt and Allison Nicholas. These people would become some of our closest friends and we regard them as our close family. The service was excellent and the Senior Pastor of the church was David Carr. We felt at home there. The Senior Pastor came over to greet us; he took one look at me and recognised me from my last church. I was surprised; I had no idea he had been to my last church, which tells you something about my powers of observation as I sat on the Board of Directors there and I did not remember him coming, and yet he recognised me.

Tanvi and I soon settled in and introduced the girls the following week; we started to go to the Tuesday services, called Legacy, as it was well known for healings to take place and there were many testimonies there that could bear witness to them.

Renewal gave us a new sense of purpose and hope, the teaching was refreshing, and yet it kept us grounded in our thinking. At no point was the teaching at Renewal feeding us false hope. Yes, people have been healed at Renewal, but there is the other side to the coin, some people do not recover, and this was clear in the teaching; there was no mistaking anything. On certain Christian channels you hear about healings and only the successful ones, but at Renewal, you get to know who had not been healed. I had to unlearn a few ideas that were contrary to Bible doctrine; we were both on a fast learning curve.

We were fortunate to get to know Pastor Dave very well, he came to visit us at our house and we spoke at length with him. By now, Tanvi was full of fight and was ready to go the distance. Going to Renewal had given both of us the spark that we needed.

SEPTEMBER 2013

The pressure started to grow and I was back in that old situation, but this time it seemed a lot more intense. This time I was trying to deal with the possibility of raising two girls on my own; those thoughts would never leave me. It is amazing how, during tough times, our thoughts can be so selfish. Tanvi was now facing death and yet all I could think of was how would I cope, how would the girls cope, how would we deal with things after? To add to all this, as a Christian, you face the constant battle of whether you are walking in faith or not. You have thoughts about how you would get on after her death and yet if you are a man of faith, why are you even having these thoughts? Are you nullifying your faith having these thoughts? Therefore, you beat yourself up for a perceived lack of faith. This is reality; it is this mental battle that you fight during grave circumstances. You tell yourself, "Stop thinking that way; have faith and trust in the Lord." Then you go to church and you are told to have faith, and faith comes by hearing the word of God. However, the battle rages on; these are the effects of turmoil in difficult situations.

Work was suffering as well. I remember one time I was doing something and I must have made a stupid mistake.

I emailed my friend Pinar and told her I was making silly mistakes and that it was getting to me. She encouraged me to hang on in there, but at that moment I felt useless. I went into the break room as I had tears in my eyes, I just needed to get away from my desk. I was broken and felt like a shell of my former self, useless and unable to function. I gathered myself and went back to my desk thinking about how this illness had broken me in ways I could not imagine. We had been fighting this battle now for well over a year but it seemed like forever. I could not remember what it was like to have a stress-free day; I could not remember what life was like before cancer; when would this all end?

One day I requested to go home early as I was struggling to deal with the situation. I knew I had to do something about it so I arranged for some counselling. I arranged to have six sessions every two weeks. Therefore, between the sessions and going to church, it helped me to deal with some of the mental battles I was going through. I suggested to Tanvi that she might need some help in this area, and she agreed. Tanvi had become very clingy at this point and I sensed the feeling of insecurity that was coming from her. Her drive to read the Bible was strong; she would spend quite a few hours on and off reading and learning. I was proud of the way she would deal with things and continued to grow spiritually as she absorbed herself in the Bible.

Being at Renewal gave us a sense of protection, knowing that the church would be there to help; we would get visits from the church to ensure Tanvi was all right. Julia would come and visit Tanvi on a number of occasions and would bring soup for her as well. Tanvi and Julia built a strong friendship; I knew they would get on, as I told Tanvi on numerous occasions. Cyrille was there also or on the phone if ever I needed advice. Bryan and Jan would offer us support as much as they could. Allison's support was there also; while Ally would say she did not say or do much, however sometimes it is not what you say; the fact that they are there standing by your side to support you is enough.

LESLEY'S TESTIMONY

Around this period, Julia suggested that we come to a meeting at church where a woman was going to speak about how she was diagnosed as terminally ill with a form of cancer. Tanvi was too ill to travel so I went on my own, meeting up with Julia and Cyrille. We sat down to listen to Lesley's testimony. I thought it best for you to read it for yourselves.

On May 29, 2002 I was diagnosed with non-Hodgkin's lymphoma, stomach and bowel cancer, this was the worst day of my life, to be told you have cancer. I wanted the truth off the doctors even though I was scared stiff to hear it, he told me my chance of survival, even with chemotherapy, was less than 40% as it was so aggressive and advanced that it could have spread further to the brain. There are two places non-Hodgkin's can go where it is undetectable that is the brain and a man's bits, his testicles. I had to start chemotherapy straightaway, which meant the next day. My whole world fell apart, in those few seconds everything going through, my head my kids my mom absolutely everything I couldn't believe this was happening to me. The doctor explained that I had to go home and tell my children as I was going to be very poorly and prepare them for what was going to happen to mommy. How can you prepare four small children for this? Connor was twelve, Rhône and Mikey my twins were ten and my only daughter Dara was eight. Can't tell them that I have cancer and may not survive so I tried to explain using every word except cancer, told them that it would be like this for them. But my oldest Googled non-Hodgkin's lymphoma on the Internet and found cancer which destroyed him. So the doctor was right, as I needed to explain it my way not the Internet way. This was then the hardest heart-wrenching thing I have ever had to do in my life. All I wanted to do was to watch my children grow up, get married and have their own family. The fear came in me, who was going to take them to school, football, Irish dancing? I was a single mom. My boyfriend at the time, Andy, was a Christian who attended a church called Renewal and they had a healing ministry on Tuesday night; he kept asking me to go, I kept refusing as I was a non-practising Roman Catholic and I thought this would be disloyal to my own religion. When you're desperate and so ill and my heart started racing, I thought why not, I've got nothing to lose and you gave everything a chance. I told Andy I would go but sit at the back of the church and as soon as they wanted my money, I would make a swift exit. I've watched too many American TV channels where they are always after your money. When I went I was amazed how many people were there, all religions and races, all wanting the same thing, healing, how desperate we all were. Pastor David Carr called all the people with *cancer to the front and Andy said to me 'Go on then'. My heart started racing, I didn't know if I could go. I was frightened, did not know what to expect. But hey, up I got, walked to the front, stood in a long line, waiting for this man. As he approached me, as I looked, I could see people falling backwards onto the floor I thought 'Is he pushing them over?' So I prepared myself standing with one foot behind the other so if he pushed I was ready for him. Pastor Dave got to me he asked me what was wrong, to which I replied I had advanced non-Hodgkin's, he anointed my head with oil, placed his hand onto my head and started praying and got everyone behind me to pray. Next thing I was on the floor, if I can explain, I wasn't knocked out. I was calm and had a warm sensation. I felt my body at peace, the most peace I had felt since being diagnosed. I was crying uncontrollably, not knowing what on earth had just happened. I got up back to my seat, sweating and crying. Andy looked at me and said while I was at the front, God told him that I would be healed. So the next week I wasn't on the back row but on the front row wanting to be prayed for, it gave me hope. I had five chemo's put through a vein in my hand which hurt like mad, plus I had to have one through the spine to get to the brain, this one was agony and I always feared if it was inserted wrongly it could have paralysed me. In all it took eight hours to do; before each chemotherapy I would have an endoscopy, this is a tube down your mouth into your stomach and they will take pictures and biopsies just to see if it had spread any further or if I was making any response* to the chemo. If I can explain, my cancer wasn't a tumour but a mass. It completely covered my stomach, black, not a bit of normal pink tissue anywhere plus it had spread to the upper part of my bowel, so surgery wasn't an option. My hair fell out instantly with the chemo. After going that Tuesday night to Renewal I went to my appointment the next Tuesday morning for chemo, they sent me down to do an ecology for my endoscopy and the doctor kept taking biopsies. It took longer than usual, I thought, will you hurry up? I hated it. I started panicking thinking what if it had spread further, or no more chemo telling me I had no hope, nobody said nothing down in oncology. When I got back up to the cancer ward the doctor explained that all the biopsy pictures were clear, there wasn't a trace of cancer in my stomach or bowel. It had disappeared. They showed me the pictures they had taken and we compared them. He said he was amazed and had no explanation as to how, but I told him that I had been to a healing church, that I was prayed for, he started smiling, I think he was a Christian. He explained that I would have to continue with my six-month treatment, as they didn't know what they were dealing with, which I agreed to. I asked if I could keep the pictures to show the pastor, to which he said yes, so I had my chemo for eight hours and stopped off at church on the way home. I rushed up the stairs to Pastor Dave's office, with my pictures in my hand, excited and crying and I didn't come up for air, explaining fast that my cancer wasn't there. Pastor Dave stood silent because he was more shocked: how had I got in, as it was *a security door downstairs and it could only be opened from the inside? I think God opened it ready for me. That night my pictures were on the big screen in church for everyone to see. The place erupted, the best thing I ever did was to give God a chance. I gave myself to the Lord, I was baptised with Andy in the pool, I was born again, the old me washed away. God gave me a second chance. I don't know why God healed me and not others, I think he thought to himself, I'm not having her up here with me she will drive me mad, or he had another purpose for my life as non-Hodgkin's isn't curable but can only be contained. Twelve years on and still cancer-free just celebrating my 50th birthday. God is still working in me; at my last endoscopy the doctor had to ask where they took the biopsies from, as all my scars from twelve years of biopsies and fifty endoscopies, the scars had disappeared. I wake every morning thanking God for letting me see another day and I pray every day that this continues.*

I was amazed and encouraged by Lesley's testimony; a sense of hope came over me. However, what struck me more that night was what happened after. We were introduced to Lesley, she asked how Tanvi was. However, next Lesley said, "Everybody asks about Tanvi, but how are you?" I was surprised, somebody was asking how I was, not as an afterthought, because that is how it felt at times, but as her primary concern. For the first time in a long time, I felt as if someone had noticed I existed. Lesley said, "I ask that because I know what my Andy went through, so I know you're going through a rough time as well. People tend to forget about how you feel, which is understandable, but you're suffering just as much." At last, someone who understood, who knew what I was going through; I felt I wasn't invisible any more. I know that was not the case and that people knew I was struggling but I didn't sense that, all I got at times was, "Be strong," and, "You're the one who needs to be strong," that was easier said than done. Andy and Lesley went on to be good friends of ours and still are to this day.

THOSE COUNSELLING SESSIONS

It was quite clear at this point that the pressure of Tanvi being diagnosed as terminally ill was too much to bear. I did not want to let it build up as I had done last time, so I sought for help from the counsellor I spoke to last time. However, what bothered me the most this time was that I was dealing with many thoughts, which made my mental state even worse. I am normally a very private person and keep things to myself; I would only reveal things about myself to people who I was close to and then again, they only got what I only wanted them to know.

There was one thought that was going through my head that was really dragging me down. I was wracked with guilt and remorse and I could not understand where it was coming from. Tanvi was terminally ill, she was going to die, and yet in my head were thoughts of whether I would ever find a partner in the future. I could not understand why that was in my mind, Tanvi was still with me and yet I was having these thoughts running through my head. I felt guilty, disloyal; I called myself a man of God yet I had these thoughts. I spent days on end beating myself up; I would at times cry myself to work and then gather myself just before I would go in. So one morning, when I was with the counsellor, I told her what I was thinking. I felt ashamed as I spoke with her. The counsellor said that I was not the first to have such thoughts and that many people go through this type of thought process; it is a way of us trying to cling onto hope in such desperate situations. I felt like a big weight had been lifted off my shoulders. She said not to worry, it's normal. Our minds are complicated and our natural instinct is to cling on to some form of hope for our future. I thought I was the worst husband going, I did not want those thoughts, I never asked for them, but there they were.

After I left that session I felt a lot better; I felt the release from her words. Those thoughts never came back after that but it is amazing how our minds can latch onto a thing and take you in directions in which you just do not want to go.

OCTOBER 2013

The counselling sessions took me so far, but we still faced the fact that Tanvi was terminally ill. Anger was an issue at this point. I was having a bad day; this would happen in waves, where I would be okay and then I would hit a dip. Now that we were going to Renewal, the atmosphere did change in the house. We spent a lot more time in our Bibles and spending time at Renewal gave us a sense of purpose and hope in Christ; however, anger and frustration would be there festering in the background.

JUDGEMENTS MADE DURING HIGHLY EMOTIONAL TIMES ARE GENERALLY THE WRONG ONES

It was around this time that unfortunately, Sandra, my friend at work, lost her father. He had been suffering from Alzheimer's and resided in a care home; looking after a loved one with this awful illness is very difficult. Sandra had been under a lot of pressure; not only did she look after her dad, in conjunction with other family members, but she ran her own house as well. Somehow, she also managed to maintain her workload; I was never able to maintain the same level of work in my situation but Sandra did; however, I could see the stress on her face at times. Sandra's dad passing away touched a raw nerve with me. It did not take long before I was full of tears; it took a while for me to gather myself.

Sandra and I talked a lot during those days and shared stories with each other, and how we were doing. One day Sandra would talk and all I would do was listen and then some days I would talk and Sandra would listen. I think it suited us both and helped us in many ways. However, after Sandra was back from compassionate leave, I noticed a change, which at the time I did not understand. Sandra would spend her lunch times with other people and I felt she seemed to be pulling away from me. I couldn't understand why she would do this and felt hurt at the time. It would be a whole year before I fully understood what was going on, and frankly her decision to pull away was not only the right one but also necessary. I can only speak for myself, but Sandra and I did speak about this after Tanvi's death and she had no idea that she had done this. Sandra was upset with herself; however, I said that I understood.

When you have spent so much time in a situation of high emotional stress and when that pressure is lifted, I tell you the truth, it is such a relief. While we may grieve for our loss, our relief from the constant pressure of appointments, medication, and mental turmoil is like having a whole planet lifted off your shoulders. Sandra was now released from that burden and she could live again and, quite rightly, my burdens were mine. Sandra deserved a break. I would realise that later on and will delve more into this later on, but for right now, Sandra did the right thing.

When we are highly emotional, we tend to think the worst of every situation and I thought Sandra was being rude and selfish and I was hurt. In hindsight, Sandra was right and she did not do anything wrong; it was all in my head. We never think straight when under pressure, so please take that on board.

Tanvi's treatment had started by now; however, it took a while to get this cleared as we were now on experimental chemo, and it needed to be authorised by my private health insurers. While it was available, it was not part of the NHS list of cancer treatments. I was not sure exactly why, but I do believe money played a big part in this, as it cost around £20,000. Thankfully, everything was authorised. Even so, the family was ready to step in to pay for the cost if necessary.

The treatment Tanvi was having would hit her hard; one of the major concerns we had to look out for was the risk of infection and a high temperature. The temperature was our main concern, as this could be a sign that she may have developed an infection. This in turn meant her white T-cell count could drop to dangerous levels and she could slip away. It was the last week of October. Tanvi was having a difficult week; her temperature started to rise, and I was in touch with the nurses. The hospital told me that I had to do my utmost to try to bring the temperature down. She had taken all the medication that we had, but this wasn't working. I had to take that whole week off work because it was quite clear she was going to need my attention. Tanvi liked to listen to Hillsong and she had a few favourite songs so I played them in the background, which made her feel good. The nurses suggested that I use cold damp swabs to try to bring the temperature down, so I did. My aunt came over to help. She brought with her some lavender oil, so I got a bowl and some swabs and placed them on her forehead and stomach. She was burning hot; she wanted the blanket but that would only insulate the heat, so I told her she had to stay uncovered. I would do this from early morning until around midnight for five days. Her temperature was so high that every time I put damp swabs on her they would come off completely dry. My aunt would help me out in the daytime so I could eat. This was a highly stressful time as I was not sure if she would pull through. I'd never felt such stress like this before; I was on automatic pilot, just doing things, I'm not sure where my strength came from. Finally, during the end of the week, her temperature started to come down. She was finally able to get out of bed; she needed help but at least she was out. This was the risk that we faced with the type of chemo she was having. The effects of her past chemo were never this severe, so this was new territory for the both of us. We started to see a slight improvement in Tanvi; however, optimism was soon replaced with the reality that we were dealing with a terminal illness. This would take its toll on Tanvi as she finally decided to have some counselling. I was pleased as I knew how much it had benefited me. Even so, Tanvi never forgot others and sent me an email at work. She wanted to pass on her thanks to my bosses for giving me the time off to look after her. This was Tanvi, and she understood the value of thanking someone.

NOVEMBER 2013 –
THOSE DIFFICULT
MOMENTS

Tanvi had started her counselling and I was hoping this would help her; however, she faced the ultimate reality: the possibility of her death. I say possibility because, as Christians, we clung on to God's healing power. As you witnessed in Lesley's testimony, it is possible but not a certainty; we knew this. Tanvi would sit up with me in bed and would read and study her Bible, while I read another book. One night when Tanvi was reading she turned to me with tears running down her face and said, "I don't want to die." What do you say, what do you do when your loved one looks you in the eye and gives it to you straight? I turned to her and said, "I know, just carry on reading the Word, everything will be okay." What else was I going to say? What else could I say? Tanvi turned back to her Bible and carried on reading. I did the same but I wasn't reading anymore. I was trying to process what Tanvi had just said; I just bottled it all in. When the lights were off I would cry quietly to myself. Every now and then, Tanvi got wise to this so she would tell me, "Everything will be ok, trust the Lord." I would reply with a flippant, "Yeah I know, I'm fine," trying to put a brave face on it all.

Julia would come and visit every now and then, bringing soup with her for Tanvi, and I was aware that they spoke a lot on the phone. We had a number of visitors from the church, which is what makes Renewal so great to be at: how they would look after us and others in similar situations. I was back at work for a short period as Tanvi insisted that, as she was able to get round the house well, there was no need to be hanging round. The cough she had developed remained with her; sometimes it was so severe and other times light, but it was there for all to hear. There was one night at Renewal when her cough got so severe during the service that she got up and walked out. She went into the reception area and went for some hot water. Normally she would come with a flask and by now, the church had set up for her a comfortable chair to sit in as well. All we had to do was to ring up and the chair would be ready.

One day, Tanvi phoned me; she had got up at 11:30 and she had just eaten, yet she felt tired. She had been tired all weekend, her coughing had increased and by now, fluid had entered her lungs. I told her not to worry and that she would be okay. What else was I to say? There was nothing else I could say and yet, as we ended the conversation, I felt my words were hollow, with no substance. I spoke to Pinar about this and as always, she continued to encourage me.

DECEMBER 2013 –
THOSE UNANSWERABLE
QUESTIONS

It was quite clear that Tanvi had a lot going through her mind; this was evident when one evening she came downstairs into the back room where I was watching a game of football. She entered and asked me if she could ask me a question, but asked me not to get angry. I realised this was going to be a question I did not want to hear. Tanvi went on to ask me if I would ever marry again. There was an awkward silence, which I ended with, "Stop asking stupid questions." I was taken by surprise; frankly, I did not expect it. I tried to act as if I was busy watching the game even though I had just lost all interest in the game. I was upset and felt, *how you could even ask me this question?* Deep down I did not want to answer, I was feeling guilty because maybe my answer would have been, "Yes, when the time is right." She went on to say, "You know, if you did, I would be okay with it, as it would be selfish of me to say no." I continued to act as if I wasn't listening, and she went back upstairs. Now I couldn't even think straight. As soon as the game finished, I rang Cyrille and told him what had happened. I told him I was disturbed by her question, he asked me why. He said it just showed that she was thinking of me and the girls. Cyrille's words of wisdom calmed me down. I just had not known how to handle it.

Christmas was coming and it was my sister's turn to host in London. I discussed with her Tanvi's ability to travel, as I knew she would have one treatment as we entered December. I was off work from 19th December and was not due back in until 7th January 2014. Tanvi was well enough to travel and we had a decent Christmas day. Little did we know that this would be our last Christmas together. I noticed a pattern in her treatment. The initial treatment would give her a boost then she would gradually deteriorate, as that particular chemo would falter.

JANUARY 2014

Christmas had gone without incident and the New Year as well. However, Tanvi was weak and it was time for more tests. This time we received the news that we did not want to hear: the cancer had spread to her lungs, which was why she was feeling weak. We were given a choice: if she took the new chemo, she would have around six months to live, if she did not she would have roughly three months. Therefore, we decided it would be best to take the chemo. We still kept going to Renewal, seeking God. We trusted our God to bring healing to our house. However, now the frustrations started to kick in. Tanvi noticed that I was not reading my Bible as much, so she encouraged me to keep strong. I remember snapping at her that I would. I felt frustrated; why wasn't he healing her? What was he waiting for? Others got healed, so I knew it did happen. I recall one evening coming home from work. Tanvi and the girls were downstairs. I threw my bag into the bedroom corner, and started having a rant at the Lord. I put a case to the Lord: if she dies, how would this glorify him? Because I just could not see it. I stood there going through it in my mind, looking for different scenarios in which God could be glorified by Tanvi dying. I wanted an explanation. I tried to reason with God. I even explained to him that, if he did heal her, the testimony would be great and many would be led back to him, as if he didn't know. I said, if he didn't, I just couldn't see what he would get out of this; absolutely nothing. After I had let off some steam, I resigned myself; I calmed down and said, "Let your will be done," and went downstairs feeling low.

That time had come again where I would once again be a bearer of bad news for all the family, letting them know she had only six months at most. You can imagine how it drags you down, each person you tell, however brave a face you put on. But all that does is bottle it up inside you, manifesting later in anger, usually towards the girls or others who are hurting as well. We decided not to tell the girls that Mom only had six months; they would only start counting down. You could see the worry on their faces, Kira especially, as she was the oldest. Kira would notice conversations around the house so we had to be extra careful to protect her and Anjali.

I rang my in-laws in India and spoke to my brother-in-law; here again, I felt the pressure of always delivering bad news. That is all I seemed to do. That feeling of being a failure came over me again; this time I felt the full pressure of their frustrations. They wanted me to bring Tanvi over to India to have treatment. They felt she would have better luck over there. Frankly, that was never going to happen; Tanvi was not allowed to travel in her condition and she was having the best treatment here. Tanvi's aunt was here with us and while they agreed with me that, okay, she was having the best treatment here, when they were speaking to Tanvi's aunt I could hear them saying that the people and the doctors don't know what they are doing and that she was better off over there.

This just compounded the feeling of failure; I felt as if they did not trust me to do the right thing, and I was stressed, but this just made it worse. I did not need this added pressure, not now. They wanted to see her files so they could get a second opinion in India so I reluctantly agreed to this. Tanvi was not happy about this. However, we agreed, but we were both fixed in our thoughts that Tanvi could not travel anywhere. Frankly, she could not even think of leaving her kids behind, and I agreed.

So, having spoken to the consultant, we sent the files over for them to check if anything else could be done. I knew in my heart that they would not be able to find anything better, but I suppose it was important for them to been seen to be doing something. It must have been difficult for them as well, to be so far from her. Therefore, in hindsight, I understand, but at the time I did not. Tanvi did understand, so I listened to what she had to say. The results? As I expected, in fact the doctors there said, not only was she getting the best treatment, but also some of the medicines she was getting you could not get in India. I felt vindicated but I understood their worries. Tanvi spoke to them and said they had better come over and visit, so plans were underway for them to see her.

GETTING YOUR
HOUSE IN ORDER

Tanvi and I now had the arduous task of sorting out our finances and ensuring that, if Tanvi passed away, life would not be so difficult going forward. Even then, we faced a battle of faith: were we walking in faith? Was planning for a life after her death an act of faith? We believed that God would heal her and yet, if that was the case, how could we plan for after? As ludicrous as it may sound this is the conversation we were having. Lesley Sparks was visiting Tanvi that evening so we asked for her opinion. Lesley must have had the same thoughts as well, and we were right. Lesley said, "God is your plan A, you getting your house in order is plan B, it's common sense that you ensure that you are all looked after if she doesn't make it, you would be silly not to." You do not think straight when you are going through tough times. You second-guess every decision; you make yourself unsure about most things. That is why it is vital you surround yourselves with people who have experience and those, if you are of a faith, who are balanced in their thinking. It is no good if you are going to be around people who are going to go off with the fairies and get over-spiritual. You need sound people, positive people, therefore choose wisely whom you allow into your life at all times.

So I arranged for both of us to go and see our solicitor. We needed a will for both of us as we didn't have one; then it was a trip down the bank to arrange for me to be given joint ownership of all her accounts. The life insurance kicked in so the mortgage was cleared. Even in situations such as this, God was still moving in our lives. For early repayment, you face a penalty fee on any mortgage; ours was £7,000. Tanvi suggested ringing Nationwide Bank to ask to see if they would waive the fee, as they were getting the mortgage paid off anyway and we needed to find this £7,000 as well. I was hesitant but as a good husband I spoke to the woman on the phone to confirm payment of the mortgage, and then put in our request to see what would happen. They had our file on record that we were paying the mortgage off due to terminal illness. Within a minute after speaking to her manager, they said, "Consider it done." I thanked them and informed Tanvi. She said, "Told you," and continued to praise God and thank him.

FEBRUARY 2014 – ANEEKA'S TWENTY-FIRST BIRTHDAY PARTY

Tanvi's new treatment was progressing, this treatment was all about giving her more time. She seemed well but that was common after every new treatment; she would react well but after a while, she would slip back. February was a month where my niece would turn twenty-one, and as we all know, it is a landmark that we all want to celebrate. Even though we had this cloud over all our lives, my sister contacted me to see if we were able to come down to London to celebrate. My sister was concerned about even holding the party, considering the situation we were in. She called us in advance, as she wanted our view as to whether she should continue to plan things or postpone it.

Tanvi and I discussed this and we felt that it would not have been right to cancel the party; you only have one chance at turning twenty-one, so we said to go ahead, we were fine with it. My sister and my niece would have been happy to go with anything we said, but it was right that she went ahead. Tanvi was not able to travel and the chemo treatment would take a lot out of her, so my parents decided to stay at home with us. However, after speaking to my brother, it was right that my girls went with him down to London; why should they miss out? Therefore, we stayed at home. To ensure we wouldn't miss out, we came up with the idea that we would Skype from my brother's phone and when they cut the cake, we would be there in some capacity. That was good but, of course, it was not the same. Tanvi and I watched as they cut the cake. I kept one eye on her just to make sure it was not too much for her. I think I felt a bit disappointed, but tried not to dwell on it too much. The whole family was there, so naturally you want to be there as well.

THE BLOOD TRANSFUSION

Tanvi's treatment continued; however, it was taking its toll on her body. We went in for one of her routine chemo days and they said they could not give her the chemo because her T-cell count was too low. They said the only way around this was to give her a blood transfusion. Tanvi had had enough. She lost her temper and threw her mobile across the room. All her frustrations came out; the pressure of treatment after treatment was taking its toll. The nurse said she would give us some time and left the room. Tanvi started to cry, saying that she had had enough, and when would this all end? I tried my best to console her without saying anything that would aggravate the situation. It was frustrating for the both of us, but I could not imagine what it was like for her. After a good ten minutes or so, she calmed down, but I knew from experience it would not take much to set her off again, so I chose my words carefully and after a while she agreed to go ahead with the transfusion. This would not happen on the same day, as they would have to bring in her blood type. We went home that day with Tanvi looking down. It was bad enough having the chemo but the blood transfusion just added to the situation. I cannot blame her for losing it; it was only the fact that she was a tough little cookie that she was able to continue on this journey.

That said a lot about her mental resolve, she was tough, my very own 'iron lady', you could say.

MARCH 2014 –
CONTINUAL TREATMENT
AND NOSE BLEED

Throughout March, Tanvi's treatment continued, we still hung on to our faith, our trust in God, that he would do well by us. We both understood that we were in a period where anything could happen. We continued to go to Renewal Christian Centre. With all the stuff we were going through, going to Renewal was still important for us, especially the Tuesdays. Tuesday night was a night of healing and prayer. Maybe this Tuesday night was our night? Maybe we would receive healing tonight? By now, Tanvi's voice had taken on a husky sound due to the constant coughing. One evening at church she was coughing so much she got up and left for the coffee area. I wasn't sure what to do, because she just got up and left. I knew she had gone to get some warm water, as that would help her to control the coughing. Most days we would come to Renewal with a flask of hot water, and she would help herself to that when she felt the need.

A woman came up to me from behind and said she was a paramedic and that she would go and check on Tanvi. I thanked her. She stayed out for most of that service in reception. Pastor Dave continued to deliver the message and pray for those who were ill. Later on, he came up to her and said, "You struggled a bit there, sweetheart." She smiled at him and he gave her a hug. I remember that loving look that he gave her to this day; it was so sweet. That is why I will always love this man. His compassion for people is for all to see, and for Tanvi, I could see it clearly. A church is only as good as its leadership. Take a look at your leader; what type of a person are they? Does their character reflect down through the church? At Renewal, it does. Does Renewal get everything right? No, but there is love and compassion there and that can only come from the leadership in place.

ALL NIGHT AT A & E

One particular day when I was busy dealing with Tanvi, I saw a window of opportunity for us to be able to finally sit down and relax. Tanvi was by the sink and she was coughing. Suddenly she called me and said, "I am bleeding." You could see drops of blood in the sink that had come down from her nose. I rang the nurse and she told us to go to A & E, so I told my parents that we needed to go to hospital, so could they keep an eye on the girls. We left at 10pm and made our way to Good Hope Hospital in Sutton Coldfield. While the bleeding had stopped, it was important to get it checked out. I had a feeling that this was going to be a long night, so I grabbed a couple of bananas on the way out. Checks were done on Tanvi that night and they found that all she did was burst a blood vessel in her nose due to the coughing. Therefore, they treated the problem and we were discharged so we could go home; it was 5:30 in the morning. I was due to go to work that day. However, I phoned in, as I was shattered and exhausted. They understood.

It's amazing what you get to see through the night at A & E. One old man was brought in with his family and they were next door to us. He was funny, kept arguing with his daughter who was well frustrated with him, as he would not co-operate. Tanvi and I did have a good chuckle at that as his daughter gave him what for and it was all water off a duck's back to him, he did not care. Those two bananas helped us. Otherwise, it would have been a tough night.

APRIL 2014 –
WALES TRIP

April had come round, and we had the Easter break. Tanvi and I had agreed that a nice little holiday would be good with the girls. Therefore, the four of us went down to Laugharne in Camarthenshire, Wales for four days; it was a lovely place and the weather was kind to us. We had a great time. The scenery was beautiful, near Dylan Thomas' boathouse. This would be our last family holiday. Even to this day it grieves me that it was our last together. I cannot help but shed a tear as I dwell on this fact. Even now, I feel it for my girls, never being able to spend time with their mother again. They didn't deserve this.

MAY 2014 –
TANVI'S BROTHER COMES
TO VISIT, AND KIRA GOES
OFF TO PARIS

Back in September 2013, Kira had come home one day with a letter from her school. They would pick around thirty students out of the whole year to go to Disneyland Paris for four days. However, the criteria was they would take the thirty best-behaved children on this trip so it wasn't going to be easy to get selected. The trip was not cheap: over £400 for four days, plus spending money.

There were many things to consider before we agreed to enter Kira. Naturally, she was keen, but Tanvi's condition would have to come into consideration. What if her mother's health deteriorated while she was abroad? How would we get her back? Even worse, what if she passed away while Kira was abroad? The last scenario would devastate her and the ramifications of that would last a lifetime. We had no choice but to think of all these things. However, we realised that we could not let the situation control us, and it would have been unfair to Kira if we had not given her the chance to enter. So I said to Tanvi, "What are the odds of

Kira getting picked anyway?" I knew my daughter; she was not the quietest in the house or anywhere, frankly, so I didn't think she would get picked. Famous last words.

One day I hear this child come screaming down the road and along the driveway, waving some letter in her hand like Neville Chamberlain declaring 'peace in our time'. I knew exactly what it was. I remember saying to myself, "You're kidding me." I opened the front door and went in the study where Tanvi was. Tanvi asked me, "What is it, is that Kira?" I said, "She has only gone and got picked for the Paris trip." Tanvi sighed and said "You're joking." Kira came bouncing into the house shouting, "I got picked, I got picked, I'm going to Paris, you have to let me go, you agreed to let me go." I said to Kira, "Hold on, calm down, me and your mom need to talk about this." She looked like she was about to cry. Tanvi said, "What we going to do? We did agree. We have to let her go." I said, "We did, didn't we?" We both had resigned looks on our faces.

If it had been any other situation we would have been just as happy for her, but this was different. Her mom was terminally ill; there was a lot to think about. However, we agreed to let her go. We could not change our minds now. This had all happened in October 2013, but now it was time for Kira to go, and Tanvi was well and in no immediate danger. I had kept the option open in my own mind to pull her out if I deemed necessary, but luckily, Tanvi was fine and Kira had a great time.

It was during the month of May that Tanvi's brother and his family came to see her. It was an emotional meeting for them. Tanvi only had one sibling so it was a difficult period for them both. They were close and it must have been hard to see your only sibling going through such a difficult time. It was good having them over as it gave me a chance to know my brother-in-law a bit better; the only time he would ever see me was when we would go over to India. Whenever we went over to India, he would always take us everywhere so it was an opportunity to take them to see places if possible. One occasion was when we all went to Drayton Manor Park and Zoo. Tanvi went along as well and it was an opportunity for her to get out of the house; she was feeling well enough to go and it was local anyway.

It was Thursday 29th May and Tanvi was starting to lose feeling in her left foot; she found it a struggle to move around near the end of the month. However, Tanvi wanted me to take her brother round London for the day to see the sights, but I was not keen on leaving her on her own with my parents. I wanted to be by her side; however, Tanvi said she would be fine so I planned a trip to London and booked tickets to do the London bus tour for 30th May. However, things sometimes just do not go to plan.

Tanvi was due to go and see the specialist that Thursday night. She did not really need to be there, so I said I would go alone and she agreed.

MORE BAD NEWS!

I made my way to the hospital. I expected it to be a routine report; however things had changed. I sat down and I was informed that she now had lesions on her brain; this would explain the lack of feeling in her left foot. She was slowly deteriorating. I asked the doctor, "What is next? What do we do now?" He said, "We have done all we can do now, we cannot continue giving her treatment, there is only so much her body can take, we have reached the end."

I sat there not knowing what to say or do. I would have to go back now and tell her. I decided not to tell her brother; I didn't want to send him back home to India with this news as he was about to fly in two days. I got home and Tanvi asked what they said. I told her we would speak later, she agreed. Her brother came to ask. I'm not sure what I exactly said but it was most likely that the routine line of treatment was to continue as normal. That night I sat in bed; Tanvi was waiting for me to tell her, so I gave her the news. For the first time in two years of her fighting cancer, I saw something on her face I had never seen. A look of resignation. She was giving up, it was in her eyes. I told her that the reason she was struggling with her movements was down to the cancer spreading to her brain. I had run out of words of encouragement. I was starting to feel the pressure even greater than before. I was still hoping, still praying; I had nothing else.

30TH MAY 2014

It was time for her brother and his family to go back to India. Tanvi and her brother spent some time alone in another room. The mood was sombre, and I did my best to focus on the trip, as I had to drive down to Heathrow. We made our way down to Heathrow; I don't think we said much. Kira had already said her goodbye to her uncle as she was now on her trip to Paris; she was due back the next day.

2ND JUNE 2014

Tanvi was now starting to feel worse. She was struggling to breathe at times. She did have a large oxygen tank in her room, which she would use every now and then, and she found it useful. The room resembled a hospital ward: tablets, hospital containers, and a large oxygen tank. We tried to read our Bibles but the pressure was heavy. I could not take that burden any more. I was not willing to go through into 2015 with this anymore. I felt I was ready to crack. I told Tanvi I was going to pray and I wanted her to agree with me. So I started to pray, "Lord, we can't take this anymore, the pressure is too great, we are not prepared to go into 2015, you have a choice now: you either heal her or you take her home." Tanvi looked at me, let out a little loving smile and nodded in agreement with the little energy she had. I continued, "Lord, I commend this prayer to you in the precious name of Jesus Christ, Amen." Now we sat back and rested. I felt I had reached a breaking point; it was only by the grace of God that I did not have a heart attack. I would shake at times with stress, we were just so tired. Tanvi took one look at me and saw that I was weak and tired. She reached out and said, "Don't give up on your faith, stay strong in the Lord always."

3RD JUNE 2014

Tanvi's breathing was getting heavier. I rang the nurses as it was late in the evening. They suggested I call an ambulance and get her into A & E again. I envisaged another all-night sit-in. However, this time when we got there she was seen within an hour. The doctor said we needed to admit her into the hospital, for tests. If I recall, I stayed with her until the morning, which took us into Wednesday 4th June. Tanvi's liver had become inflamed and there was pressure on her heart caused by water that had gathered around the area. The plan was to operate and draw out the water. Even at that point, I was still hoping, not even thinking that we might lose her. The thought did not cross my mind. That would later come to haunt me.

Throughout the day, Tanvi got weaker and weaker, to the point that she could hardly speak. Kevin Thomas and Tom Kemp, two good friends, visited her from my church; they prayed for her. I was so focused on what the doctors were going to do, I just did not see what was coming. I went home that day and brought my mom with me to see Tanvi. Around 8pm it was time to go. I said to Tanvi that I would be back to see her in the morning. She couldn't speak but just looked at me. Oh, how I wish I had stayed. The guilt that I did not stay with her that night I carried for a long period. Even now, nearly two years on, I have tears about that night.

THURSDAY 5TH JUNE 2014

I went home that evening. The girls wanted to see their mom. I said that, once everything was sorted, then I would take them in. Therefore, we all went to bed. I kept the phone by my side just in case they needed to contact me.

It was 4 in the morning when the phone rang. I answered. "Mr Naik, this is the hospital." I asked if everything was all right. "You need to come in, your wife is poorly." I asked again "Is she all right?" "Mr Naik, you need to come in, your wife is poorly." She said it twice; something was wrong. I said, "Okay, I'm on my way." I got out of bed and stood there, I composed myself and immediately rang my brother. He knew I had taken her in, he said he was on his way. I had a quick shower; I don't know why, I just did. I got out and as soon as I got downstairs, my brother turned up. I informed my parents we were going and left. We didn't say anything to each other. Deep down, I knew, but I needed to see for myself. I needed to hear the words. We went in through A & E. I looked at the staff and they just looked at me. Their faces told a thousand words. I still wanted to hear for myself. We went up to the ward. We were asked to wait in a room: more confirmation, but still. The doctor came in. He seemed to have the weight of the world on his shoulders.

He started to speak, struggling to start. I was shaking at this point, so I thought I would put him out of his misery. I said to him, "She's gone, hasn't she?" He said yes. My head sank; he carried on speaking about how they tried to revive her, but to no avail. I said, "Can I see her?" He showed me into a room and there she lay at peace. I sat by her side; I leaned over her in tears. "I failed you, I didn't do enough, and I should have prayed more, I should have fasted for you more." I felt a deep guilt all over me, my brother consoled me. He said I did everything I could as he cried with me. I felt so useless, such a failure, I could have done more, why didn't I do more?

There was a chair next to her, so I sat down. I searched inside of me. I felt empty. Was I angry? No. What about God, was I angry with him? No. I said, "Let your will be done." She looked so beautiful lying there. Two days before, the girls had painted her nails in red. I rang Pastor Dave and he came straight away. Ten minutes later, I rang Dad and told him. I left it to my brother to ring everyone else. However, it was my duty to ring Tanvi's brother. I and I alone was going to tell him, there was no shifting the responsibility on this one. My feelings at the time were, *I brought her here to the UK and I was responsible for her safety and I failed, so stand up and be counted.* I rang him and told him.

Pastor Dave came in and we embraced. I asked him, if we prayed for her to come back, she wouldn't, would she? He said... "No." We sat there for a few hours, the three of us. Pastor Dave would speak to her every now and then; they were such soothing and loving words. He would look at me and say, "Look how great she looks." I would smile at him.

We were coming up to half past six in the morning. I knew the girls would be getting up for school soon, so I needed to be there. I took one last glance at her and left her with Pastor Dave by her bedside. Now the big question was, how do I tell the girls? What do I say to them and how? We got back home and my sister-in-law and my aunt were already there. I called the girls down. Kira had sensed that something was wrong. She came down the stairs asking, "Why are all these people at our house? What is wrong?" I sat them down and told them their mom had gone home to be with the Lord. Kira broke down, and so did Anjali. It was the toughest thing I have ever done.

After a while, Pastor Dave turned up at the house. He stayed with us for most of the morning. It was comforting to have him there and he was so loving with the girls. Kira decided to stay at home but Anjali said she wanted to go to school. I wasn't quite sure about that. My cousin Sheila was there, who is a trained counsellor dealing with children. After consulting Pastor Dave and Sheila, we thought it was best she went to school, as it was her happy place. I was a bit concerned for Anjali, as she didn't grieve the way Kira did. I know they are both different but I expected more tears from Anjali; she was acting as if nothing had happened. Kira tended to wear her heart on her sleeve, you got the full works with Kira and I could handle that, but Anjali was very different and I found that hard to deal with. I had already informed the school about the situation and they were more than happy to have Anjali at school, so Sheila and Tom, a friend from church, and I took Anjali to school. Anjali just talked as if it was a normal day. I wondered if it had really struck home, what had just happened, and maybe she didn't understand. I proceeded to ask Anjali if she understood what had happened to Mom. That question was met with an angry short sharp response of, "Yes I know." She understood, but was dealing with it in her own way. Having Sheila there was helpful. Her skills as a child counsellor were invaluable and, more importantly, Sheila had been through the same thing when she was the same age; her dad passed away through illness as well. During times like these, you cannot help but feel history is repeating itself; it was difficult for all of us.

That day was a day when the whole family pulled together. My sister came up from London, each person you met brought up different kinds of emotions. Pastor Dave left around 12pm, I think. He has always been there for me and still is.

THE FIRST NIGHT ALONE –
WOMAN OF GOD

As the day went on, I knew I would eventually have to go into my bedroom. The girls were being looked after, my sister stayed with us and other family members would only be a stone's throw away. I felt for my nephews and nieces. My eldest nephew found it difficult to face the girls; I am sure they all did.

It was night and time to get some sleep. I did not want to go in my room but I had no choice. It was tough; I felt as if I would rather be anywhere else but in my room because it had been our room and now it was not. I quietly went about getting ready for bed. However, for some reason, I just stopped and asked the Lord, "Lord, do you have her?" Then as soon as I said the last word I heard the last end of the scripture from John 3,16, *"For God so loved the world that he gave his one and only Son, that **whoever believes in him shall not perish but have eternal life in him"**.* I responded with a slight smile and a clenched fist, "Yes, Lord, Glory be to God".

You see, you might think: is that it? Not much of a confirmation. Well, actually it is all we need. The Lord was never going to say, "She is right here by my side." We have to remember, a walk with Christ is always a walk of faith-to-faith. Remember in Hebrews 11, 6 it says *"and without faith it is impossible to please God."* That is only part of that scripture. I knew that I would have to take a leap of faith to believe. Tanvi loved the Lord; a few days before she passed away she encouraged me to stay strong in my faith, not to give up. To this day, that will always amaze me; her body was tired and battered but her love for the Lord was strong, and her spirit was strong. I tell you now, she shook the gates of hell with those words, she knew she was going home to be with the Lord, she was victorious in death as she was in life, and to this day I will always be proud of her.

THE LONGEST NIGHT

I had settled it in my heart: she was now at home, at peace. I never questioned the Lord since that night as to why he hadn't healed her. What was the point? Was knowing going to bring her back? No.

I got into bed that night and sat there in the dark. I stayed on my side of the bed and, to this day, I still do. I could not sleep, and I did not want to do anything else, read, watch telly, nothing. So I just sat there in silence staring ahead. Every now and then I would glance over to her side of the bed and just stroke where she would have slept as if I was comforting her. I stayed up until 3am, just staring ahead; there was a completely numb feeling about the situation. I did this for the first week and struggled to sleep for the first month.

FRIDAY 6TH JUNE

I eventually got to sleep, I don't really know what time it was but next day I sat down with my brother and we started to list all the things we needed to do. Visitors were aplenty that day, which was expected. However, funeral arrangements needed to be done, death certificates needed to be got, no time to sit around. First, I wanted to go and thank the nurses at the private hospital, so I took them a box of chocolates. I felt comfortable when I got there, it was familiar ground. I didn't go on my own, I was never allowed to; my family were always with me wherever I went.

Little did I realise the impact going back to the hospital would have on me. The woman who was in charge of the hospital saw me and did not want me to go home without seeing her. I went in and gave them the chocolates but as I left there was this strong feeling of not wanting to leave, it was painful and very strong. For some reason, I felt as if I was leaving Tanvi behind, the pull on me not to leave was so much I broke down in tears. This place had become our second home; we spent so much time there that it became a part of us, it was a part of me. She was still here and I did not want to go home. That is when reality kicked in: she was gone. It was at that point that I realised Tanvi was dead, it was at that point I started to grieve. It has been nearly two years now and I still have not been back there. I have driven past a few times and always glance that way but have never been there since. It was that day I mourned her death.

FREEDOM FROM THE
BURDENS OF CANCER

Tanvi's passing away also did something for me; I was released from the burdens and worries that came along with cancer. Now I understood what my friend Sandra must have felt like, the relief of not having to think of appointments, visits etc. Now I knew that Sandra was right because, frankly, I was not interested in anyone's problems, even the Macmillan adverts got on my nerves. I just didn't want to know.

LEAD UP TO
THE FUNERAL

My brother and I started to sort out the funeral arrangements, and I was asked what type of funeral I wanted for her. Tanvi and I were both Christians so, naturally, that is what I wanted. My brother and my sister said whatever I wanted, they would honour and support me all the way. It is not as if I was going to get some dissent among the family, but they wanted me to know that they were with me all the way.

For the funeral there was only one person I wanted, that was Pastor Dave. I wanted to keep it in the family, my church family. I also asked Arvel Lowe, an elder from the church, if he would be my funeral director as that was his job. He agreed, so that was it, I had my home family and my church family; it was going to be family and no one else.

TANVI'S PARENTS
FLY OVER

Tanvi's parents were going to come over to see her; unfortunately, they did not make it in time. However, they agreed to come over for the funeral so I delayed the funeral for an extra week. I did not want to because I wanted to get everything out the way. The gap between the death and the funeral I call 'No Man's Land'. You can't go back and you can't move forward; your life is placed on hold until you get past the funeral. However, I felt the decent thing to do was to wait, to give them closure.

I wanted a Christian funeral but frankly, I had no idea what happens or what kind of ceremony I wanted for her. Therefore, my brother and I went to see Pastor Dave at Renewal and worked things out. Pastor Dave asked me what I wanted, I told him, "To be honest, I don't have a clue," so we discussed having three speakers. I could possibly be one, if I was capable, if not, Pastor Dave would speak on my behalf. Julia was close to Tanvi so it was easy for me to ask Julia and she agreed. In addition, I asked Adrian Gill, a Director at HSBC Bank, who she knew well and who she saw as her friend, and he agreed. Therefore, I had everyone lined up. I asked the girls if they would like to write a little poem or message for their mother, to which they agreed with smiles on their faces; they were pleased to be a part of the service.

I had one final request: a song, our song. I used to play this song to her during her time at home when she was recovering or going through a difficult period. The song is by Hillsong United Oceans – *Where Feet May Fail* – we loved this song, so it was set that we would play this at the end. Everything was ready and it was time now for her parents to arrive.

On the morning of their arrival, I was tense and agitated; the only person who noticed was my sister. I would snap at people, they would just take it as they thought I was just grieving, however there was more to this. How would I face my father-in-law? What would I say? That overwhelming feeling of failing their daughter was eating away at me. I did my best to keep myself busy but I was always clock-watching. My brother went down to Heathrow to collect them, it was agreed by all that it was not best for me to be travelling. They would not arrive until around eight in the evening, so every now and then, I would watch the clock and as time drew closer, the tension in me would rise.

Finally they arrived; the emotions in me were at tipping point; her father and mother were grief-stricken and struggled to enter the house. Finally we met, we embraced, and I managed to contain my emotions for a bit longer as they sat down. My parents and my aunt were in conversation with them. Tanvi's aunt, who I was close to as this was one of many trips to the UK, was standing next to me. Suddenly

I broke down, sobbing heavily, she held me in her arms and as all the emotions came flooding out I said, "I tried my best but I couldn't save her." All the day's emotions that had built up inside of me came out in one go. I could not contain the guilt I was feeling; I had failed her, and I had failed them. Tanvi's parents spoke and said there was nothing I could have done, and those words comforted me.

What was I looking for? Was it acceptance, was it some form of acknowledgement that I had done my best? Was I expecting some form of frustration and anger from them, telling me that I did not do enough, or was this something deeper in me that needed to be exorcised?

I have recently been on a counselling course where we discussed how, over time in our lives, whether we do it to ourselves or others around us do, we establish 'Conditions of Worth'. For example, if a child throughout their youth is told they will not amount to much in life, as they grow older they develop a 'Self Concept'. What this means is they will develop a view of themselves in which the only way someone will accept them is if they try hard in life. So their whole aim and goal in life is to keep pushing themselves. That is their 'Condition of Worth'. A negative view has fashioned their way of thinking and is now a motivator for them in life or possibly it may have a negative effect on the person, causing them to become withdrawn and lack confidence.

Did I place a 'Condition of Worth' on myself regarding the way my in-laws viewed me? Did this explain my feeling of failure or thinking I had let them down in some form or another? This view certainly did not come from them as at no point did they ever convey this to me. Or did I pick up this view from my own values and expectations? Yes, there was the time when they asked me to send her report over to India, but all that did was to place a brick on a foundation that was already there. I believe I still have this condition in me as I have often thought that, if I were to marry again, I would get it right: a drive in me to be a better husband. The question is, what was wrong in the first place?

19TH JUNE 2014 –
THE DAY OF THE FUNERAL

The day of the funeral had arrived; it was a lovely warm day and everything was ready. The service was to take place at the Streetly Crematorium at 3pm. I knew the service would take some time so I booked in a double slot, and we were the last service in. I was pleased about that as I did not want to overrun into someone else's time slot. I have been to funerals where that has happened and frankly, it's embarrassing and out of order. The order of service was as follows:

Opening prayer
Rt. Revd. Dr. David E. Carr

Tributes
Adrian Gill
Julia Regis
Prashant Naik

Address Rt Revd Dr. David E. Carr
Committal

Music
Hillsong UNITED Oceans (Where Feet May Fail)

While I was down on the order as a speaker, I just could not do it; I am a highly emotional type of bloke, I just knew I would not last the distance. I decided to sit with my girls and Pastor Dave spoke on my behalf. I was amazed at how many people turned up, especially her colleagues from HSBC, it just showed the amount of respect that people had for her at work; it was standing room only. The service was beautiful, all the speakers spoke with dignity and with such respect. However, the most moving part of the service was the poems my girls wrote; these were read by Pastor Dave.

To Mum,
I wrote this letter because I know you'll be listening. I know you know how much I love you, but I want everyone else to understand how much I do. During Mum's treatment, the doctors said she was full of life, that's how I knew how **STRONG** my mum was. In this room, everyone knows how **STUNNING** my mum always looked every day. Hopefully Anjali and I will grow up looking just as **BEAUTIFUL** as Mum. When I was revising by myself I didn't get the marks I wanted but when I revised with Mum I achieved a level at school that I never imagined I could. That shows how **CLEVER** my mum was. My mum was the **BEST COOK** in the world and when my friends came over they always asked to go home with a margarine

tub filled with mummy's homemade Indian food. My favourite was her Chinese chicken legs and no one can make it like she did. Mummy was a very **CARING** and **GIVING** person, she always picked me up when I fell, put a smile on my face when I was sad but the best thing about her was her hugs and kisses. Thank you Mum for taking care of me for these 12 years and have a nice life in heaven. I love you so much!

Love from Kira xxx

My Mummy is…
My mummy is kind,
My mummy always has a clever mind.
She always gives the bestest hugs and says I ♥ you,
My mummy is very cuddly and fun to play with too.
My mummy is very strong and in my heart, she belongs.
She always watched the programme Trendsetter and when it comes to fashion, she is always better.
Ever since I was born,
Mummy always gave me my favourite veg, corn.
So bear in mind my mummy is the best mother in the universe and that is something I will always remember.
Love from Anjali XXX

The service finished with our song; it was very moving and touching. I will never forget that day as long as I live and beyond.

We drove back in the funeral cars and made our way

home. Arvel was driving the car I was in, which made me feel my church family was with me. We set up a collection box and on the day of the funeral, we raised over £1,000, which was gratefully received by the Macmillan charity. Now the time had come to move on, to start a new chapter in my life, but that is another story. The Unknown Journey.

TWENTY-TWO
MONTHS ON
NO MAN WALKS ALONE

We are coming up to nearly two years now since Tanvi went home to be with the Lord. It has not been an easy journey, full of grief and sadness. I look back over the two years of treatment and sometimes wonder how we got through it all. I say "we" but it is not "we" any more, it is just the girls and me. I sometimes look back and wonder, was she ever with us? Were our sixteen years of marriage real? There are times when it feels like it was all a dream and she was never with us, but then you get a glimpse of a picture and you remember a moment and that moment comes rushing back to you. It is the girls I really feel for. I am forty-nine years old, I still have both my parents with me, and yet they have lost their mother at such a young age. This is what I struggle with, the injustice of it all for them. However, you cannot live like that; you have to move forward, as hard as it may be. My focus has to be the girls and their well-being, there are times when I may be too strict on them, as they remind me every now and then. Tanvi and I had ideas about their education, and how we wanted to bring them up, and I still follow that plan. I am constantly surprised how strong my girls are and how proud I am of them in handling the cards they have been dealt. Yes, they miss their mother, and at times are frustrated with Dad's efforts of juggling both roles, but I know they will be okay, by the grace of God.

My biggest struggle is dealing with loneliness. There are times when I am fine, however, some days it is a struggle. I believe you never get over a loss like this, you just adjust, and as time goes on you learn to adapt. The girls and I are still at Renewal and it is amazing how the Lord works at times, because I now run a Men's Bereavement Group at the church on the first Saturday of every month. We are a group for men who have experienced loss of any kind; we are committed to helping each other as we navigate life after loss.

FORGET THEE NOT

Added to this we also have the long-established Ladies' Bereavement Group called 'Forget Thee Not'. This group is for women only who have experienced loss of any kind. They are committed to supporting each other as they share their experiences. The women's group meets once a month, on Saturday mornings at 11am, for coffee and cake.

You are welcome to join us. We meet at:
Renewal Family Centre
Vulcan Rd
Solihull
B91 2JY

For more information, contact us on:

0121 711 7300
or email church@renewalcc.com

LITTLE FINGERS – NEVER ALONE IN THE SHADOWS

One of the most moving books I have read recently is a book called *Little Fingers*, written and compiled by Charlotte Nall.

Taken from *Little Fingers'* back page:

"This book covers one of the most painful experiences anyone could ever endure: the loss of a child. It is during this time that parents feel overwhelmed with emotion and grief that they are not sure if they will make it through the days ahead. Many people look for places of support in a desperate attempt to navigate their way.

Little Fingers: Never Alone in the Shadows aims to be a resource that intends to bring light to the questions a grieving parent will face after the tragedy of losing a child, as well as point them in the right direction of support services available to them in the coming weeks, months and years. This book aims to be a companion to help you through the coming days that lie ahead. Our aim is that **you are never alone in the shadows!**"

MY VIEWS

While this book covers grief from different perspectives, and we all grieve differently due to our uniqueness, I have found that different types of loss can and will overlap. There are many similarities within *Little Fingers* I can point to, and it was easy for me to think that this book was for me after losing Tanvi. Loss is loss, whether it's death – human or pets – or divorce, it is still a loss. I have not covered my grieving process in my book, but Charlotte Nall has done a fantastic job in covering some of the aspects of her grief and just as I did, I'm sure you will be able to visualise your own loss in an inspirational piece of work. This book is available free for bereaved parents from *www.littlefingers.org.uk* and contains many other helpful links as well.

Church Service times:
RENEWAL CHRISTIAN CENTRE –
Lode Ln, Solihull, B91 2JR
http://www.renewalcc.com/
Please join us at Renewal, you are more than welcome.

Our services are at:

S1 – 9.00am

S2 – 11:00am

S3 – 1:00pm

Or on Tuesdays at Legacy at 7:30pm.